Jumping Into Empty Space

Jumping Into Empty Space

A Reluctant Mennonite Businessman Serves in Paraguay's Presidential Cabinet

by Ernst Bergen
as told to Phyllis Pellman Good

Intercourse, PA 17534
800/762-7171
www.GoodBooks.com

The experiences presented in this book reflect the opinions and observations of the author. A few of the names have been changed to protect the privacy of certain individuals and their families.

All photos supplied by Ernst Bergen, except photo on page 204 by Merle Good.

Design by Cliff Snyder

JUMPING INTO EMPTY SPACE

International Standard Book Number: 978-1-56148-654-0
Library of Congress Catalog Card Number: 2008041574

Library of Congress Cataloging-in-Publication Data

Bergen, Ernst.
Jumping into empty space : a reluctant Mennonite businessman serves in Paraguay's presidential cabinet / by Ernst Bergen as told to Phyllis Pellman Good.
p. cm.
ISBN 978-1-56148-654-0 (pbk. : alk. paper) 1. Bergen, Ernst. 2. Paraguay--Politics and government--1989- 3. Paraguay--Economic conditions--1954- 4. Cabinet officers--Paraguay--Biography. 5. Mennonites--Paraguay--Biography. I. Good, Phyllis Pellman - II. Title.
F2689.23.B47A3 2008
336.892092--dc22
[B] 2008041574

Contents

Introduction 3

Part I—The Story

1. What the Public Expects of a Public Figure 7
2. Learning Self-Control 16
3. Doing It My Way 25
4. Figuring Out Business and Investing 34
5. A Vision for the Party Leaders—and for Me 42
6. Trying To Say No 47
7. Why a Convinced Business Entrepreneur Reluctantly Joined the Government 62
8. Attracting Good People 73

9. Finding My Way 84

10. Keeping One Foot in the Church—and in Prison 93

11. Behaving Well, But Communicating Poorly 99

12. Staying Sane 109

13. Seizing a Moment 119

14. Power—And What to Do About It 126

15. Itaipú—An International Sore Point 130

16. Seeing the Big Picture and the Little Picture at the Same Time 138

17. Deciding to Leave—Without Knowing the Future 154

18. From Intensive Care to Intermediate Therapy? 170

Part II—Behind the Story

A Brief History of Paraguay 177

About the Mennonites of Paraguay 181

Paraguay Country Brief, September 2006 186

Statement by an IMF Staff Mission to Paraguay 190

What We Set Out to Do 192

Ernst's Letter of Resignation 199

About the Authors 204

Introduction

On August 15, 2003, Ernst Ferdinand Bergen became Minister of Industry and Commerce in the government of Paraguay. He served at the invitation of Paraguay's President Nicanor Duarte Frutos.

After he held that position for 21 months, Ernst was asked by President Duarte to become the country's Minister of Finance. That post is perhaps the most beleaguered spot within the government. Paraguay is a developing country and has two great needs, among many: to legalize its fiscal practices, and to bring relief and opportunity to its many poor people, including its large farming (*campesino*) class.

Ernst served in that position from May 19, 2005, until July 30, 2007, the longest tenure of any Finance Minister in the last three governments.

Ernst Bergen's grandparents were German and Polish Mennonite refugees who found a home in the Paraguayan Chaco as World War I ended. Ernst grew up in Filadelfia, Fernheim, a Mennonite colony situated in the inhospitable wilderness of the Chaco. He had no interest in government or politics. He was part of a highly industrious religious people who, for reasons of history and theology, were acutely suspicious of being involved in government.

This is an accounting of how and why, at the age of 39, Ernst Bergen became a trusted confidant of President Duarte and reluctantly joined his government. In his two cabinet-level positions, Ernst helped to begin an important financial and economic recovery for the country.

This is the story of that remarkable turnaround in Paraguay's financial footing and of one impatient, but conscientious, business entrepreneur.

Thank you, Ernst, for inviting me to help you tell your story. I'm still astonished by your honesty and self-awareness.

Thank you, Alfred and Wilma Neufeld, for tirelessly translating my questions (asked in English) to Ernst, and his answers to me in Spanish and German. Thank you, too, for bringing us all together in your home in Asunción in July, 2007, where the idea of this book was born.

—*Phyllis Pellman Good*

Part I
The Story

Chapter 1

What the Public Expects of a Public Figure

Dealing with the press was not my favorite part of my job. I did have several staff who helped me with this daily task.

One morning I arrived at my office in the Finance Ministry around 8:00. My agenda was full. I was meeting with Laura, my press chief, when Dario from the press department interrupted our conversation. He looked worried and he spoke in a tone of despair. He informed us that one of the victims of the Stroessner (Paraguay's long-time dictator) regime, an elderly man, had climbed up the tower of a local Asunción radio station, Radio Trinidad. He had climbed to the top—262½ feet from the ground.

He was asking to speak to the Minister of Finance, or he would throw himself from the tower.

Laura's phone began ringing, but she didn't answer it because she never took phone calls when she and I were meeting. But I signaled with my eyes that she should attend to her phone. It was a radio station reporting from the scene. She put her cell phone into my hands, with the radio station live on the air. She thought I should calm down the population and the situation. The idea was that I would speak to the radio station, and their reporter would speak to the man. Meanwhile, Laura informed me, the press and TV cameras were on their way to the station.

I said, "What do I do, Laura?"

She thought maybe I should address the man directly.

Barely hiding my sarcasm I said, "We have lots of towers in this country. Should I encourage others to climb towers so they can talk to me?"

By then, a crowd was gathering around the tower. The radio station announced that it had the Finance Ministry on the phone. Laura convinced me to talk on her cell phone. I tried to use my most reconciling voice, all the while trying to focus my thoughts on the Bible's statements about the value of each human life.

I was live on the radio. I heard myself saying, "The life of Juan is very important to all of us. Our greatest concern is to help Juan come down so we can discover what his demand is. Then we will try to be helpful within the Ministry and the framework of the law."

The radio director said, "So, you're on the way? We can expect you within a few minutes?"

I replied, "I'm trying to understand Juan's anxiety. It's my highest intent to give him just treatment. If our Ministry has been unjust, I want to learn that from him. I guarantee I'll listen to him so that I can understand what's gone wrong.

"And could he give us more time so that we can figure out the appropriate response since I don't know his real needs? When I have a clear picture, I will try to be helpful."

People on site communicated my message to Juan with a megaphone. Meanwhile, I called in my team and asked them to help me analyze the situation. I also called Félix Duarte, the chaplain of our church's prison ministry, and asked him what to do since he was experienced in crisis intervention. Félix suggested that first I should require Juan to come down, and then promise to receive him immediately.

Laura stepped into my office to say that TV cameras and several radio stations were at the tower, along with others Juan had asked to be witnesses: the ambassadors from Cuba and Venezuela; Mario Melanio Medina, a bishop in the Roman Catholic church; a public ombudsman; and Hermes Rafael Saguier, one of the most polemic, well-known lawyers in the country. Juan had invited the Cuban and Venezuelan ambassadors especially because their countries represent the political left, as does the Roman Catholic bishop.

I called state security and Rogelio Benítez, the Ministry of the Interior. "There's a special crew for these kinds of incidents, and they are approaching the tower now," said Benítez. And security said that I should talk with the guy *after* he came down. "Tell him, 'I'm leaving the office; you can start climbing down.'"

I cancelled my meetings with sugar producers and with U.N. authorities and headed out of the office. And I asked my one Vice Minister, Miguel Gómez, to go with me to the tower. He had already gathered background on the man. President Duarte had instituted a program that pays benefits to victims of Paraguay's earlier dictatorship. Juan was among the 511 persons who had received reparations from this fund. The Vice Minister informed me that we could legitimately make another payment to Juan and other victims of the dictatorship.

"How would this not lead to others climbing towers and making similar demands?" I shot back. We drove slowly to the site. I saw towers everywhere, and I was sure I saw people on all of them! I was tempted to tell Juan to jump so they would all see the danger of his approach.

Thanks to the expertise of the security teams, and to Juan's cooperation, we convinced Juan that I was on my way and that I would talk to him once he was down. When I got the message that he was down, we stopped slowly driving around. I arranged a private meeting room. But Juan's supporters wouldn't stand for that.

When I arrived at the tower, everyone stuck mikes in my face. I asked to talk first to Juan. We went to the meeting room, but about 15 other people insisted on being with us—Juan's family, his militant lawyer, the bishop, the ambassadors, the ombudsman, the owner of the radio station. I entered with my Vice Minister Miguel, a master at administering crises. Security had to force the door shut. I sat down beside the old man, looked into his eyes, and asked, "How are you doing, Juan?"

Of course, I was the bad guy. Naturally I was upset. First I thanked everyone present for being so cooperative and eager to save Juan's life. I assured them that I was there to find justice and a solution, and I asked for their help. Juan was crying. I asked the group to be attentive while Juan told his story.

I think Juan realized that I was trying to be reconciling. First, he talked about suffering under the dictator Stroessner and the injustice he experienced. Finally, he began to talk about yesterday evening, right before the tower event. He had had a bad moment with his daughter who needed money. He had nothing to give her. Then the propane gas tank for cooking was empty. His wife sent him to buy propane, but he had no money. Now he was a failure in front of his daughter *and* his wife. He couldn't sleep the whole night. So he decided to do something important for his family. He wanted to vindicate himself as a father and husband with guts.

What should he do? He got the tower idea. He would publicly claim the just treatment that he wanted but never got from Stroessner. Now here he sat, upset and crying with his wife.

The expectation inside and outside the room was that I would make a big commitment. I said that I understood his feelings of having been unjustly treated. I thanked him for climbing down. I assured him that others, too, had suffered as he did. The Vice Minister and I had talked with the leader of this organized group of victims, who were also in the room. We had been able to help these victims a lot in the past. "We are all touched by this situation," I said. "And we are all tense. In fact, we might be in danger of making decisions that are unjust for the rest of the victims. The important thing right now, Juan, is that you saved your life and came down. Juan, I invite you to visit me at 8:00 tomorrow morning in my office, and we will decide the next best steps. Bring whomever you want with you. Together we will find a solution."

He accepted that, although some of the others who were present didn't. The next big challenge was facing the press outside. I proposed that my Vice Minister face the press and tell them that we would find a resolution tomorrow, and that we would brief them after the morning meeting. The whole group rejected that idea and insisted that I address the press immediately.

I said, "Okay, I'll speak to the press, but I will not take questions." I asked the roomful of people who had come to witness my conversation with Juan to understand this tense moment, and to remember that our responsibility was to the whole country and to *all* the Stroessner victims. We dared not harm others as we sought a solution for this one.

There was lots of pushing on the way into the press conference. It was totally chaotic. All the mikes were open; the press was shouting constant questions. I greeted the whole group. I said, "I am happy that Juan is alive, and I will turn the mike over to him." Juan was emotionally moved. He indicated that he agreed with what we had talked about and was happy to continue the process.

I took the mike back to give my perspective but to answer no questions. I thanked Juan for his trust and the others who had contributed to our negotiations. I asked Juan and the others present to please understand that governments must work within the framework of the law and that our solution must be available to all victims of the Stroessner regime. I underlined the importance of those who fought for liberty and justice during the Stroessner years and since. Then I thanked them all, hugged Juan, said I'd see him in the morning, and stepped out. The journalists followed me with their questions.

I wanted to convey the message that we in the Finance Ministry would solve our problems internally, and on our own schedule, and not whenever someone used drama to pressure us.

The incident reinforced an important understanding for me. Leaders tend to make unwise decisions when they are under stress. Through God's grace we managed this situation, and I was thankful that I hadn't lost my temper or self-control. The next day we were able to settle the matter in a legally proper way and to Juan's satisfaction. But Juan threatened that if I cheated him, he'd climb the tower again!

The tenser I am on the inside, the calmer I appear on the outside. It wasn't always so. In fact, it's been a long and sometimes grievous growing process for me, rooted in some experiences of failure. A story from an influential, international agency's inner workings helped me early on. Some main players in the agency faced a big decision and needed to respond quickly. They gathered for a meeting. The guy in charge started talking about the coffee they were all drinking. For 35 minutes they talked about the quality and quantity of the sugar and the coffee. And then, in less than 10 minutes, they talked about the issue at hand, and they were able to make a good decision together because they had all calmed down.

"Sugar in the coffee" became a code word in the Finance Ministry. I'd slip it into conversation when my Vice Ministers and I were in a difficult meeting, and they knew to make small talk until things calmed down.

I discovered that the heat in a meeting didn't need to draw down my energy, if I could stay focused on my objectives and strategy. And I made a point of not being insulting with my tone of voice and body language while holding firm on a position. I should have figured that out earlier in life!

Ernst (second from left) greeting President Lula da Silva of Brazil (far right).

"The world leader whom I learned to appreciate the most was President Lula. I met with him at least 10 or more times, sometimes for extended periods. On a recent trip to Paraguay, he addressed business and political leaders. He opened with a humble and self-critical statement, saying that the people expect a message other than blame from their leaders. Instead, they want leaders who own their own problems because they're the only ones capable of solving those problems. Brazil is the largest and most powerful country in Latin America, and as leader of that country, he approached the Paraguayan people with respect. He urged them to solve their own needs; he said they had the capacity to do that. He encouraged people to do their own homework for the problems they were facing.

"President Lula is known to have chosen an extraordinary team of cabinet members. He insists that anyone in government must understand how politics work. Technical ability is second to that. So he chose various specialized technicians who understand very well how politics work.

"He influenced Nicanor significantly on that point. I learned that I had to understand how politics work in order to succeed at my job. When Lula was talking this way, Nicanor would interrupt him and say, 'Listen, Ernesto, this is for you!'"

Chapter 2

Learning Self-Control

I was not a stellar student in school. Simply getting to the next grade was good enough for me. *Vati*, my dad, always wanted me to have good teachers—and strict ones. I found creative ways to get away with doing as little as possible. I just had no interest in school.

On the other hand, bicycles, and later motorcycles, intrigued me greatly. And I had lots of relationships and friends, and doing things with them was very important to me. I played an implicit leadership role among my friends, something I was hardly aware of. They were good people, but I often influenced them in a negative way.

My one close friend was the son of an important leader (the *Oberschulze*) in our Mennonite colony. We both thought life in Filadelfia was very boring. There were small artificial lakes behind our school that had dried up, a perfect place to try out our motorcycles. Dried-up brush filled the dried-up puddles. To prepare a runway for our cycles, we set the brush on fire one day after school, and the whole colony came to look. My dad was responsible at that time for public order in the colony. In other words, he was our Mennonite public security system. He and his assistant launched a major investigation to see who had set the brush fire, but they never found out. No one died, but it was a dangerous thing to do, and it became a pretty public scandal. We used to hear from our parents, "You are too young to know certain things." We (my friend and I) agreed that our parents are still too young to know some things!

We were required to go to church every Sunday. But I wasn't too interested in that either because the main thing we heard there was to keep quiet. As we got older, we learned there were more fun things to do. We came up with a simple plan. We young guys sat near the back of the church, out of view of our parents who sat further front. As church was beginning, we'd quietly go outside, passing by the back windows to see who was preaching that Sunday. Then we could answer our dads' questions at our dinner tables. When they asked us about the morning worship service we'd each say, "You know, Pastor So-and-So is pretty boring so I didn't listen very well, but he was preaching something about God." We'd mention one or two things we were sure the preacher had said because we knew the various pastors and their individual themes pretty well. But of course we had been out driving around.

And because we knew all the public-order people were in church, it was a good time to break the 30 km (18–19 mph) speed limit.

Most of us had Fräulein Bräul, as a schoolteacher. She was 60-plus, single, and very strict. Everyone feared her. We thought she took out her frustrations about being alone on her students. She had been trained in physics, math, and art in Soviet Russia. She was very efficient! She was also very boring. Math and art were her whole life.

My drawings and art were pretty poor, and I figured out ways to escape her assignments. When she discovered that I had mostly blank sheets, rather than completed art projects, she got angry, hysterical really. She made me stand up in class and scolded me very harshly. "How can someone with such an industrious mother be such a lazy guy?" she bellowed. She hung my blank pages around the room for all

Ernst and other students of Fräulein Bräuel (fourth from right in the back row). Ernst is in the front row, second from right.

to see and gave me a deadline for completing all the assignments I hadn't done. The next week was the deadline, but I had more important things to do! I had to find a solution. I visited her favorite, most eager-to-please students, and I explained to these girls the complicated situation I was in.

I appealed to their Christian sense of mercy, and they handed over their "lesser" work to me since they only turned in their *perfect* work. The next day Fräulein Bräul came immediately to see my work. I looked as worn out as I could. The girls whose work I used trembled with fear—far more than I did! Fräulein Bräul said, "I know his mother; I knew what he was capable of!"

This kind of behavior in school gave me a transcript that wasn't too encouraging. It wasn't clear that I would be promoted to Grade Ten. My future in high school didn't look very promising. I was much more fascinated by technical things. I had completely rebuilt two motorcycles, and that made me of interest to the other young people. I also wanted a beautiful girlfriend, and I wasn't sure I would find her in the Chaco.

In those days, motorcycle rallies were very popular. My parents didn't let me drive motorcycles in rallies, so I specialized in tuning up the bikes so they'd go faster, and mine often won. My friends had the fastest cycles because I had "prepared" the cycles to their fullest capacities. And they were very talented drivers. Of course, that's why they were my friends!

One day before a big rally, we tried out the machines. We were very excited; we went far over the speed limit, so my dad (the Mennonite sheriff!) fined us for that.

Ernst (left) on his motorcycle in the Chaco.

My young group of friends, who were competing against professionals, won that day on the machines I had prepared. We were very respected by those kids in the colonies who liked to play the edge.

By this time I was after a girl who was very pious, and I found myself in a serious conflict. My high-school grades were poor, my social life was chaotic, and I was in love with a girl who was a good Christian.

The Technical School of Caacupé, sponsored by the Swiss government, was an agro-mechanic school in eastern Paraguay, several hundred kilometers from where I lived. It was run with an almost military discipline. In fact, the school's students fulfilled their military service requirement by attending there.

It was not common — in fact, it was highly exceptional — for Mennonite kids to leave home at 16 years of age. Convincing my parents to let me go to Caacupé when I was 16 was very hard. I was happy, but my life was very disordered. My mom cried with frustration and concern about me. My dad said, "Whatever you do, I will always be your dad."

Dad went with me to the school, a more than 300-mile bus ride on mostly dirt roads. The place had virtually no communication system with the world outside. The school staff took me to the dorm—one room for 30 guys, all bunk beds, military-style with little personal freedom. I was the only Mennonite. I spoke German and didn't know Spanish well. My culture and customs were vastly different.

And I had brought along my practice of imposing things the way I wanted them to be.

My classmates had no interest in a Mennonite who tried to tell them what to do. I was soon in conflict with most of them. I was impulsive, and they enjoyed provoking me. At the top end of my bed was the head of a very big guy who always made fun of me. One night around 10:30 when he had tormented me so that I was upset, I grabbed his neck and pressed very hard. The guy became limp. The dorm became very quiet. I loosened my grip on his throat. We weren't sure he was going to survive; it wasn't clear what was happening. For five to 10 minutes he didn't really breathe. Instead, he made strange sounds. "In this crazy way, I hope you got the message," I finally said in poor Spanish. None of the 30 guys said anything. I didn't sleep at all that night. I was afraid they'd kill me. My only wish was to wake up the next morning alive. Fortunately, all of us did.

After that, people looked at me differently. I gained some respect from the others. But I had a hard time learning to live cross-culturally. I was beginning to think of going back to the Chaco, but I didn't know how to return without seeming like a failure. I kept comparing my own German immigrant culture with the Paraguayan culture. I couldn't say one was better, although my mom is a brilliant cook, and at Caacupé we were fed two *galletas* (slices of dried bread) and *cocido* (yerba tea) for breakfast. That is the breakfast of the poor.

It turned out to be fortunate that I was forced to identify and appreciate the Paraguayan culture at the age of 16. The drastic culture shock I was experiencing made me re-think my faith and relationship with God.

I graduated from that school two and a half years later, and I went back to the colonies to do a teaching practicum. I was invited to be an instructor at the highly-regarded vo-tech school in Loma Plata. Funny thing was that I became an instructor to my former friends there. They considered me to be an important guy!

When I finished the practicum in six months, the school administrators invited me to come back as a full teacher when I completed my training. I had had a very good return to the Chaco. I went back to Caacupé to take the final exam and finished second in a class of 28. But the most important thing I learned there—and it helped me a lot in my future—was *poder de contención*, a popular term now in Paraguayan politics. It means the power of self-control, of self-discipline, of not allowing my emotions to tear me away.

Ernst (left) carrying a flag at the vo-tech school in Caacupé. He received the flag-carrying honor because he graduated second in his class.

As I neared the end of my time in Caacupé, I learned to know a good family in Asunción, and especially a girl in that family. Suddenly, I was no longer interested in Loma Plata and the position being held there for me. Instead, I wanted to move to Asunción. I had to find a way to get rid of my teaching commitment in the Chaco. The Mennonite colonies were very competitive with each other, and Fernheim Colony wanted to eventually make me principal of the Loma Plata vo-tech school, an institution co-sponsored by the three Chaco colonies, because of my skills and the leadership they thought I had.

I had promised to come back to teach, but I decided to make a point of not wanting to be responsible for the dorm. The school administrators always linked teaching positions and dorm supervision. Teachers were expected to also serve as dorm supervisors. I figured that if I said I wouldn't take the dorm responsibility, I could be released from both.

The man who chaired the three *Oberschulzen* (Presidents) of the three Colonies called me into his office and told me that I *had* to come back and that I was required to take care of the dorm as part of my assignment. I agreed to honor what I had promised—which was to teach—but not more. He threatened that my refusal would be a negative point on my résumé. (My future wife Lucy's uncle was the *Oberschulze* who said that to me!) I still preferred to go to Asunción. Furthermore, I had decided that I wanted to study business administration at Columbia University in Asunción.

I called Walter Neufeld, a good friend who was a Bible school student (and also did lots of crazy things), and asked him to register me at the University. He took my high-school transcript to the registrar, who noticed that I hadn't finished my high-school humanities classes and that I'd gone to technical school. I told Walter he had to convince the University that my technical training was as good as humanities classes.

Walter managed to register me because he convinced them that "it would be a great benefit to the University to have Ernst." They would not want to miss the opportunity of having me!

"Friendship is sometimes more important than truth," Walter said to me. He used his whole rhetorical repertoire to convince them that I was a much sought-after instructor, and, naturally, a highly desirable student!

Chapter 3

Doing It My Way

My mother, Herta Schmidt Bergen, often said, "Boys, don't expect things to fall into your lap from heaven. You'll have to make your own effort and do your own part."

From my father, Heinrich Bergen, I learned that one's bank account on earth is not as important as what one has on deposit in heaven.

Both of my parents are nurses. They weren't well paid, so they also had a herd of cows to sustain our family.

We lived in Filadelfia which, in the 1960s and 1970s as I was growing up, was a little village. It is the center of the Fernheim Colony and sits in the northwest part of Paraguay in the Chaco. The cows grazed outside Filadelfia. We boys drove them into town to milk them. The cows brought in more income than my parents' hospital salaries.

My parents' account at the colony's Co-op store was usually in the red. My brothers and I had direct access to their Co-op account, which operated by an internal credit system so that we could buy indiscriminately. My parents were generous. They didn't keep track of every penny. We young people lived pretty well!

"What you sow, you will harvest," my mom would say. And, "If you want to achieve something in life, you must depend on yourself." *Mutti* is the hardest working woman I know. She instilled the principle within us that nothing comes without effort.

She taught us how to pray; she introduced us to Christian faith. She absolutely believed that we must do our part and that God will do his part. If you get positive results, it is because God has been gracious. She still feels that way. In recent years, when people have asked her, "What did you do so that your boys found such wonderful wives?" she says, "It is the grace of God. It's not something we did!"

Ernst's parents, Herta and Heinrich Bergen.

My dad has a big heart for others. When he was young, he risked his life by befriending the Ayoreos, an indigenous group who terrorized the whole central Chaco during the 1950s. Oil men from the U.S. had been shooting these indigenous people, and when two local Mennonite missionaries, together with two Christians from the local Lengua tribe, drove out to offer the Ayoreos gifts, one of the visitors was killed by the Ayoreos. My father went out to befriend the indigenous village.

Vati, my dad, clearly had a special love for the Ayoreos. When I was young, we often had an Ayoreo family living in our yard. I frequently ate armadillos with them. My father enrolled in a class to learn their language.

Vati was the first volunteer in Paraguay to work with Mennonite Voluntary Service. He worked in a state-run neuro-psychiatric hospital in Asunción, a terrible place, and risked his life there.

I see God tracing a pattern here. My dad as a young single felt called to work as a nurse. Later, he had a son, my next-younger brother Horst Uwe, who worked in that neuro-psychiatric center for a number of years as an intern while in training as a psychologist. And many years later, my wife, Lucy, along with Paraguay's First Lady, sensed a calling from God to give those with severe mental needs the highest priority in their charitable work, again in that same hospital.

Vati invested his life for others. Service was his central drive.

Mutti often complained about *Vati*. "He'd have two pairs of pants," she'd say, "and an Indian man would come along without any pants. *Vati* would just give his one pair away. How could he do that?"

My mother comes from a family with a strong ability for earning money. Her siblings achieved considerable wealth in the Mennonite community. And she knew how to make money. In fact, she put up money to build a pharmacy. Now my dad saw to it that others benefited from her earnings from the pharmacy! So she never achieved the same kind of wealth as her family.

But in recent years she says, "I can't understand how we have such a good life. We don't own much, but we have a good life. We have more than we deserve and we are very happy." Since my brother, Holly, and I both live hours away in Asunción, we are thankful that our youngest brother, Helmut Dieter, is keeping our parents company in Filadelfia.

Ernst (far left) with his family: *Mutti* (Herta Schmidt de Bergen), Helmut Dieter, *Vati* (Heinrich Bergen), and Horst Uwe.

This year again *Vati* called me, asking to borrow money. I can't hurt his dignity, so I said, "I will lend it to you, but on the condition that you pay no interest." When the date that the money was due to be repaid came, he said, "There's still a piece of our land near your property." So I said, "Okay. I'll take the land instead of the money." I suspect he gave the money away, but I didn't ask.

My childhood home was solid. My parents have been an inspiration. My family has had a major impact on who I am. They are a part of my cloud of witnesses, including my brother, Horst, whom we call "Holly." He's been the pastor of our church, which has put him in an awkward spot sometimes, especially when the President asked me to serve in his government. But Holly and his wife, Norma, are two of my best friends. They know me well—and they tell me the truth.

In March, 1983, I began taking evening classes at Columbia University and working days at Record Electric, a sizable electrical contractor in Asunción. I was feeling confident about what I had to offer. After all, I had scored well in the training school in Caacupé, and I was a much sought-after instructor in the Mennonite colonies.

But Record Electric put me into a crisis. I had to start at the bottom in a new place. In fact, I became the clean-up guy in the service department. Record Electric was in the process of slimming down and selling out because the owner was moving to Canada.

Meanwhile, I had started a private parallel business, and I employed a friend to run it for me. We bought spare parts for cars and sent the parts to a garage belonging to Walter Stahl in far-off Filadelfia, which did repairs there. I was earning much more doing that than I was making at Record Electric. So I decided not to be a mechanic, but to work the commercial side since there was more money there.

As the owner of Record Electric phased back, he put a new CEO in place. The new guy decided to open a branch elsewhere in Asunción and asked me to head that up. We did well there and became so successful that we began to compete with the mother location. Soon, the CEO called and asked me to be the chief of sales for the whole company. I agreed and moved my office back to the home site.

For the first time ever I had to re-orient employees to a new vision. They had all been going along comfortably, but the outfit was absolutely outdated. When I asked for the inventory of the motors in stock so we could re-order, the warehouse manager told me to go count them. When I objected, he got so angry that he threatened me with a knife, which he held menacingly, because I had confronted the company's normal way of doing business. During the next several months this elderly manager told me, "Don't forget; I have less to lose in life than you do." I began to understand that I needed to learn more about how to work with people. I realized that *I* was part of the problem.

That's the moment when I encountered the importance of leadership. I signed up to take a Dale Carnegie course on human relationships. Those classes, plus what I was learning on the job, helped me become successful in that firm and to get employment offers from elsewhere. I was beginning to learn more about self-control, and I was discovering that sometimes injustices happened that I couldn't change.

One day I told Record Electric's owner that it wasn't so appealing for me to work hard so he could become richer. I said I would find it much more attractive to be an owner. And so I became a minority shareholder.

As I was buying into the company, I was also working to convince Lucy Giesbrecht to marry me. This took some careful effort.

At the age of 16, I had left the closed Mennonite community in the colonies and, after studies in Caacupé, ventured into the big city of Asunción with very little preparation. At that point I was quite adventurous and not at all holy. I wanted a girlfriend with the same character and style as I had.

But now I had gone to the other extreme and found a "nun!" Lucy acted quite distant, and she had what seemed to me to be impossibly high standards. She wouldn't let me kiss her for a whole year! This caused me profound suffering, and I couldn't even tell my friends because they would have laughed at me. No one could conquer her; she wasn't approachable. But I liked her way of being. I felt secure with her. She is a very stable person.

Lucy was training to be a nurse. When she finished with that, she planned to go to medical school, *and then* maybe get married. I wanted to see if I could move the wedding date up considerably. So I went to my very wise pastor. Of course, I chose him very carefully out of the menu of pastors we had in our church. He thought that when young people are away from their parents and are dating seriously, they should marry as soon as possible. That fit with my way of thinking.

I haven't often prayed so fervently in my whole life. So with the pastor, the Lord, and myself, we convinced Lucy to move the wedding up. But Lucy had two conditions—that she could finish nurse's training and that she'd get an automatic washing machine. In 1986 in Paraguay, an automatic washer was a true luxury.

As we approached our wedding day, the very wise pastor told me, "Support everything your bride would like. Make sure she is happy." To this day I work very hard to do that!

We were married on February 1, 1986. I met Lucy's two conditions. She continued in nurse's college for three more years, and she got the washer. And I have never forgotten our pastor's words. Everyone involved in the First Lady's Foundation, of which Lucy was Vice President, will testify that I still try always to submit to my wife's happiness!

Ernst and Lucy on their wedding day, February 1, 1986.

I had found a wonderful wife, and I had become a mechanical and entrepreneurial whiz-kid. But I was still an adolescent when it came to respecting and relating to others.

Lucy's father was Jacob Giesbrecht. He was quite successful in a lumber business and in real estate. In fact, he became the *Oberschulze* for a term in the Fernheim Colony in the Chaco. My beloved parents-in-law had a beautiful house in Asunción. It stood empty as our wedding was approaching because they were living in the Chaco at that time. I thought it was logical that Lucy and I would live in their Asunción house. But one evening shortly before our wedding, when Lucy and I were visiting with her parents, her dad told us that he had just rented the house. I almost fell off my chair. How could he do that?!

I thought we would probably get the house as a wedding gift. Instead, he gave us $500. That was it. Then I realized that the Giesbrechts had given me their daughter—but their money was theirs. It was important that I learned how to earn my own living. Whenever my father-in-law has lent me money, I have had to pay the same interest as everyone else. He has shown me much, and he has become a close friend and advisor in my businesses.

Chapter 4

Figuring Out Business and Investing

Once I began to grasp the importance of managing and working with people, I started to figure out how to run a business—and grow it.

Record Electric was going well, but it had inherited a way of operating that was not completely legal. It had a sort of "double accounting" system, which was very common in Paraguay then, because it seemed to be the only way to survive. In fact, it was the ordinary course of business.

I worked my way up in the company. As I was about to become vice-president and an influential shareholder, I had a long internal struggle. I concluded that at a definite moment, I would institute a drastic change. From then on, everything would be done properly. My decision was outside the normal reference points in our country. But trusting in God, I decided to do it—and I did it. I had to convince the other shareholders, and they agreed. We have operated legally ever since. The other owners understood that they would eventually have to make this change, but to do it, courageous leadership was needed. It meant that we earned less. But I would have re-adjusted things even if it led to losing the company.

Every day before making the change, I knew that what we were doing was not always right. I was beginning to comprehend that it's not the most important thing to be the richest guy in the graveyard.

My conscience was well formed in my home and in my church as a child. About the time I was considering this change, I stepped up my involvement in our church's mission committee, especially its prison work. I became quite involved there, learning to know good people who had made mistakes at some moment in their lives. I saw clearly that I could have made these kinds of mistakes. Working with prisoners moved me closer to making this decision in my company and doing what I knew I should.

I talked a lot about these things with Lucy. She has a lot of capacity to know when to speak and when to be silent. She knows how to ask good questions. Our conversations—and her strength—helped me a great deal.

As my interest in business grew, the only limitation I imposed on myself was not to join any business that could harm. When I was considering entering a new business, I first analyzed whether the person who approached me to be his partner was capable of running the business successfully. Sometimes these were my employees; others were friends; some had a dream and asked me to join it. At times I initiated the invitation. Usually we partnered because they wanted more than an investment from me. They wanted the experience I could bring and the advice I could offer.

Sometimes I was the largest investor, but it was never my primary aim to become the majority shareholder. So sometimes I loaned others the money to invest or increase their investment. I did that in order to get a higher commitment from those who would lead the business and to show that I trusted them. That strategy has worked well. Today one of these businesses has become bigger than my original business, Record Electric. In each of the businesses that I've been instrumental in starting, I've built the structure around the person who would run the business, the one who I thought could do it. I never started by analyzing the market, but rather the *person* who could lead the company.

During the last four years while I've been in the government, I've distanced myself from the businesses. Prior to that, I wasn't very close to the operations, although I was very close to the strategic planning, and I coached the leaders who would implement the plans.

During the last few years, I've worked to install a professional board of directors in each of the businesses. I've wanted to remain a shareholder but with a professional board overseeing the operations. I have not charged any honoraria for my role.

I get great satisfaction from seeing people grow and progress. And I've earned good money as a shareholder, and that is fun, too. God has given me a gift to "accompany" business people. I enjoy that.

Along the way I've concluded that in those companies with which I'm involved in direction-setting, I will only work with Christian leaders. I've sensed God leading me in this, but God has also shown me that I should not judge others who choose to do differently.

I have friends with other convictions. I was in several companies with non-Christian shareholders and proprietors. When I decided to be directly involved only in businesses with Christians in their leadership, I had to give away my shares in one company. I couldn't sell the shares because the company was going through hard times. I spoke to several of the shareholders and asked if they would accept my shares as gifts, and they agreed to do that. Since then, despite having some very attractive opportunities, I have not become an owner of a company where the major shareholders (those who can affect policies) are not Christians.

On the other hand, I may buy shares in publicly traded companies on the stock market, as long as those businesses don't harm human health or the environment.

I wasn't always a calm and reasoned leader. In 2002, Christian Business Persons of the Roman Catholic Church of Paraguay chose Record Electric as the model business in their national award contest. It was a real honor for the business and for me personally.

During that time I was opening more businesses and I was under too much stress. I went to visit one of my mentors, Vicente Donini, from Jaragua do Sul. He is one of Brazil's most successful businessmen. I was overwhelmed time-wise and emotionally by trying to do too much. I found Vicente sitting in his office—with his thousands of employees—giving a whole day to listen to me in a relaxed way. He also took me on a tour through his factory. His employees greeted him with a smile; there was an atmosphere of tranquility.

I hoped he'd give me a list of practical suggestions. Instead he said, "You should take a one-week seminar in Brazil offered by the Don Cabral Foundation, followed by a three-week seminar in the U.S." I thought, I can't do that. My firm will collapse. He said he'd recommend me so I would be accepted. I was completely frustrated when I left.

I went to the beautiful Camboriu Beach in Brazil, about 120 miles away, where Lucy was waiting for me. Lucy wondered what the wise man said. I told her, "This guy is crazy. He gave me recommendations that are completely out of focus. But they do intrigue me." Immediately Lucy said, "Take the seminars. That's a great idea!" Now I was boxed in by two crazy people. But I realized that the way I was running the businesses wasn't going to work long-term. So I figured, if I'm going to lose the businesses anyway because I'm exhausted and overwhelmed, what did I have to lose by taking this seminar?

I had to go through an entrance interview despite my background of considerable success. I failed the interview.

The guy giving the exam said kindly, "It will not be possible for you to participate in this group, but I can offer you a course for smaller businesses." This was a tough blow for me, and I really felt like throwing in the towel. But I registered for "Marketing and Management of Human Resources," a four-week course. The Don Cabral Foundation is one of Brazil's leading consulting institutions for leaders.

During the first week, all the participants were brought to the same level. We were given two months of reading to do. The next step was intensive training at the Kellogg Foundation in Chicago for three weeks. The first thing I noticed was that the businesses I was leading were certainly not the most significant among those represented in the group. I learned to know people with far bigger businesses who were relaxed and enjoying their lives. I realized that I was extraordinarily ignorant. I began to understand the importance of surrounding myself with good people who are qualified to do what I am not capable of.

When I got home, I called together the presidents of the various companies I was involved with to talk to them about what I had learned. First, they complained about the national government, as we all have typically done. I said to them, "We business people benefit *most* from our weak government. We have no foreign investors in our country, so we domestic businesses can get away with being mediocre, sluggish, and lazy."

Some got a little scared. We determined that all the firms we owned and operated would enroll in PAEX

(Partners for Excellence), a training program sponsored by the Don Cabral Foundation that has achieved a lot of success. PAEX begins by teaching presidents of companies and then offers instruction down through the staff.

We began with two days of training sessions per month for the presidents. It turned around the way we did business. We were able to professionalize our businesses and to begin to operate internationally. We began to use international standards of excellence, so important if Paraguayan businesses are to excel within the country, as well as to do business outside of Paraguay.

I had learned a lot about professionalizing my businesses. And I had companions who also wanted to run things with integrity. But I had a big question on my heart. I participated in major businesses, but inside I felt incapable of fully living up to the challenges. Why, I kept asking myself, do I have these businesses? They

Ernst making a business contact with a businessman in China.

were considered to be model businesses, but I was nagged by the question, What is business really for? What is the meaning of business? I wanted a simple statement as an answer.

Finally, after a time of prayer and seeking counsel from several people, I came up with this phrase as my reason to be in business: "Growing Together in Order to Serve." *Crecer Juntos Para Servir.* We immediately attached this slogan to Record Electric. Whenever the company name appeared, the catch phrase did, too, and still does. And I tried hard to implement it practically, to make it reality. We began to make it possible for all our employees to have access to chaplaincy services. We started housing programs for many of our co-workers so they could build their own homes. We offered school scholarships for their children and stipends for families so they could buy their school supplies.

I believe firmly that as a business grows, its staff should benefit by growing, too. Furthermore, as persons grow in their positions, they should think of ways to enable others to grow and to eventually take their places. I believe that practicing these principles made it possible for our businesses to grow quickly—and solidly.

Chapter 5

A Vision for the Party Leaders—and for Me

No question, I love the thrill of business. But as my companies grew, I was drawn to helping create a solid economic footing in our country. Increasingly, I wanted to live and run my businesses responsibly. Being a quality leader was more and more on my mind. I wanted to do something beneficial, to make a contribution.

In 2002, when I had no idea I would someday step into government, I got a phone call from Nicanor Duarte Frutos. He was campaigning to be the Colorado Party's candidate for President of Paraguay. It turns out that he had asked around for someone with credibility in the economic community who could explain the financial structure of the Mennonite colonies in the Chaco. The

Cooperatives there operated quite efficiently and successfully, and Nicanor wanted to explore if anything from that approach to economics could be applied to the country as a whole. Furthermore, there was rumored to be oil in the Chaco, which only heightened interest in that area.

I didn't know Nicanor very well. That didn't keep him from being direct. "I want someone to help me transmit the vision of the Cooperatives to the party leaders. I want them to understand and know how to implement the cooperative system, and I want them to understand the possibility of oil in the Chaco. I will call you to my weekend home in Atyrá within a week. I would like you, and anyone else you'd like to involve, to develop these two themes for these men."

I was scared. My impulse was to look for experts who could intelligently discuss these two topics because I wasn't prepared to. But the more I thought about Nicanor's out-of-the-blue request to talk to his party leaders about the economic system I had grown up in, the more I believed that I needed to address a larger, more important, question with them.

Nicanor was trying to organize his party. He was hoping to create a unifying vision which the party could rally around. Nicanor believed that if the party leaders were convinced of this vision, they could energize the whole country, beginning to lift it out of its impoverished, fractured, hobbled circumstances.

I had read about a poll of young North Americans who were asked, "Whom do you admire so much that s/he is your hero?"

I had analyzed the opinion expressed by a majority of these young Americans, and I agreed with it. And so I prepared a PowerPoint presentation for Nicanor's gathering that I titled, "The American Hero." We got together as planned, and I was asked to speak. I told them that this hero had five characteristics that might be important for us in Paraguay. This leader asked one thing of his team, and he promised them four.

The commitment he asked of them was to follow, to stay close.

Then he made these four commitments to his team:

1. I will give you a clear objective.
2. I will speak your language.
3. I will be responsible to help you become professional in your job.
4. In critical situations, I will stay out in front and cover you.

It turns out that these young North Americans had chosen Jesus as the hero they most admired in all of history.

The party leaders were very surprised that I talked to them about Jesus. I highlighted the Bible verse in which Jesus called his followers to be "fishers of men." And I went on to develop the themes:

- "Come"—effective leaders call people to a larger vision.
- He spoke so that his followers could understand. "Fishers of men" was their language and their imagery.

- Jesus never threw blame around if his disciples didn't do their jobs well.
- "Follow me"—effective leaders reassure their people that they can have confidence in them, and they don't let their people down.

At that time, the party leaders were totally involved in an internal political campaign. I said, "Why don't you take Jesus as a model? Our people don't know who to follow. Aim to communicate as simply and clearly as Ronald Reagan did. He told the electorate that he knew what they cared most about: family, work, neighborhood, freedom, and peace. People felt understood by him, and they knew where he was going, so they gave him their trust and followed him."

Ernst and President Duarte in conversation in Asunción.

My presentation was brief. I was sweating and trembling because of the fear, but also the respect, I felt for my audience. When I finished speaking, Nicanor asked me to repeat the presentation to the whole group.

The party leaders went on to consider how the Cooperative system in the Mennonite colonies might be adapted to the whole country. Several experts had carefully analyzed how they work and were able to lay out clearly the cost and time that would be required to implement the system throughout Paraguay.

The political leaders eventually rejected the idea of adapting the Cooperative system to the whole country. They wanted fast results, and the leaders in the colonies had estimated that it takes 10 years to see positive results with the Cooperative system.

Despite that conclusion to the meeting, I had had the opportunity to sort out my own understanding of appropriate leadership as a result of Nicanor's invitation and the patience of the party leaders.

Chapter 6

Trying To Say No

The Presidential election was held on April 27, 2003. Two days later, the newly elected President, Nicanor Duarte Frutos, invited Lucy and me to his *quinta*, his weekend house in Atyrá about 30 miles outside of Asunción. We took our two-week-old son, David, with us. On the way we worried that we would be the only guests and that Nicanor would ask us to commit to some position within his government. We were relieved to see lots of cars in the parking lot when we got to the house.

When we walked in, about 30 persons were there, so we relaxed. It was an election celebration which the President's wife, Gloria, had organized. She had invited a Christian band to play. We felt comfortable. The event had a Christian, almost Mennonite, atmosphere. Gloria is a member of a Mennonite church, a sister congregation to the church we attend. She and Lucy had learned to know each other by working together on some joint church projects for women.

We tried to sit far away from the President, but he spotted us and asked us to come sit near him. We had hoped to stay on the edge so we could observe and survey. We knew almost no one, but he asked us to sit right beside his closest friend.

We made our first steps to try to fit into the new environment. The place was filled with Christian music, Paraguayan folk music, stories about election day. It was very relaxed. Then Nicanor got up, tapped my shoulder, and said, "Come with me, Ernesto." He was wearing dark shorts, a red T-shirt, and beach shoes. We went out across the lawn into the darkness.

He looked at me and said, "Ernst, I want you to be my Minister of Industry and Commerce (MIC)." I remember replying, "Mr. President, you are totally insane!" Immediately he said, "Yeah, yeah, that's the way you Mennonites are. You are very good at sitting in the bleachers and watching a soccer game. You are willing to criticize what's wrong with the government. You throw rotten oranges at the players who make mistakes. In fact, you seldom applaud the good moves."

He went on and on with a dramatic critique of the Mennonite function and role in Paraguay. I was fast enough to say, "Mr. President, let's get serious. If you think a Mennonite should take the job, I have another candidate for you. He is better prepared, he speaks English, he has stronger businesses, and he has several brothers in his businesses who can run them while he serves in your administration. Plus he has a lot of experience relating to government, and he knows well the relationship between industry and government."

Nicanor replied, "But I want you to be my minister."

I finally persuaded him to invite the guy I suggested. He gave me a week to try to convince my acquaintance. He mentioned that one of his friends knew my candidate well and that he would ask him to try to persuade the guy, too. But he went on to say, "I'm anticipating that your candidate won't accept, so I'd like you to continue to think about serving in my government." After a week, the President called to inform me that my candidate had not accepted—which I already knew. So we started talking again about the possibility of me becoming his minister.

I asked the President for two weeks to think it over. That wasn't easy for him to grant since he was under pressure to complete his team. (There are now close to four months between the election and the inauguration to allow more time for a new administration to make all its appointments.) But he gave me two more weeks.

I tried to consider the invitation responsibly. I told myself that I needed five groups to say "Yes" in order for me to agree to take the position. I had divided my social environment into these five groupings. On the emotional level I was fearful and not at all motivated to accept. But I knew I had to assess things seriously.

First, I considered my relationship to God. I asked God to give me internal peace whatever the decision.

Second, I wanted to know what my family thought. What would be best for them? I was especially concerned about Lucy and our children—Daniela, who was then 13, Samuel, who was 10, and David, who was one month old. But my parents and my two brothers were important, too. I wanted them to accompany this decision. I wished Lucy would just make the decision and that the rest would go along with it! Of course, I wanted my parents and my brothers to bless the decision. But clearly Lucy needed to be at peace with whatever the outcome. I knew that a "Yes" would bring a completely different life for our family.

The third group were the businesses I was part of. Certainly, if my businesses went down while I was Minister of Industry and Commerce, my credibility would be damaged.

The fourth group were my friends. If I entered government, I would absolutely need good friends, and I would especially need their support when I faced crises.

The fifth group was my local church. It was of primary importance to me. I considered it crucial to have the blessing and support of my congregation in this decision.

I should clarify why all of this was so jarring—no one had ever been called from the Mennonites in Paraguay to the status of Minister in the national government. This was a cabinet-level appointment.

Mennonites, who had suffered extremely in Russia in the early decades of the 20th century, had looked after their own self-government in the Chaco for years. That was part of the agreement with the government of

Paraguay when they settled as refugees in the country's wilderness. For the most part, Mennonites, especially those with a clear Christian profile, had not been involved in political leadership outside their own colonies. Those few who had participated to some degree faced crises, including relating to their congregations.

I did hear from another group, not my close friends, who alerted me that Nicanor would use me for three months, and then throw me away once I had served his purposes.

Amidst the considerable confusion of those days, I found it helpful to think of these five primary groups as I tried to sort out my decision. I had some friends, I still have them, whom I call any time and say, "Please pray hard for me, because I am not so good at praying. I'm not very effective." These friends are apparently closer to God, so I delegate praying to them. And they do their duty!

This whole strategy within myself was to find peace about *not* becoming the Minister. I was looking for a "No." A few things attracted me to the position, but they were minor. My prevailing attitude was that I was not interested. At that moment, my life was in an optimum situation. I felt at peace, useful in what I was doing.

Now came the answers.

Lucy turned a blank check over to God. She said, "If this comes from God, he will give us the strength to do it. So we must see if this comes from God." I didn't like her answer. I wanted her to say "No!" so I could say, "My wife says, 'No!'"

My parents promised me that if I took the commitment, they would support me, but that I shouldn't take the job if I didn't want to.

My mom was sitting in the yard when I called to tell her and to ask what she and my dad thought. She told Lucy later that the day before I called, she had had a kind of vision, and she isn't the kind of person to have visions! She had a feeling that the Lord said to her, "I want to use your son; I want to take him away from you." She said, "No way." This happened three times. Then she perceived God saying, "Would you oppose my will?" At that point she said, "Okay, take him, but protect him." She was crying, she told Lucy.

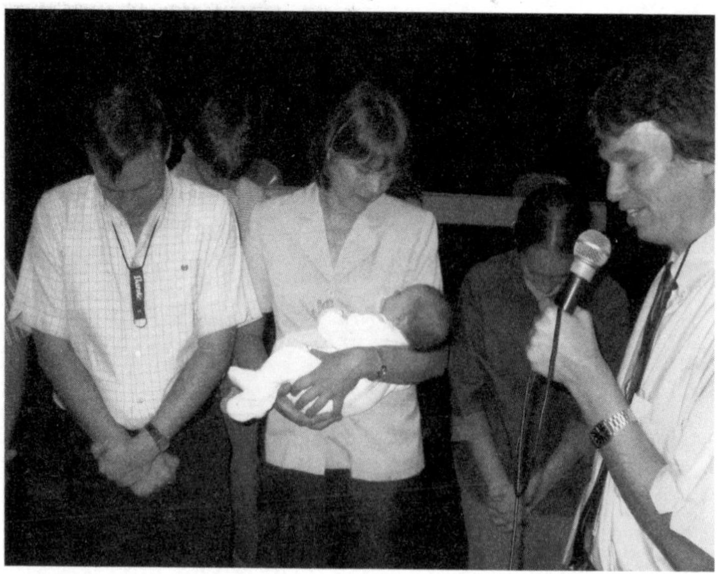

Ernst and Lucy at the dedication of their son, David. Ernst's brother, Horst (far right), pastor of their congregation, officiates.

In that moment she didn't have the courage to tell my dad, afraid that he'd think she was crazy. And that kind of reluctance is not her usual approach! It was sometime later that she told us about her visions. So my parents were willing to give me their blessing to take the position—if I felt at peace.

I was president of one of my businesses at that moment, but I knew that I had a good chance of finding leadership successors within the staff. My team was willing to step in, aware they were facing a double challenge. They would take over the leadership of the company, and they would immediately be exposed to scrutiny from the public because my business involvements would be widely reported.

I loved the businesses I was in, and I had a special struggle with God concerning them. I knew some businessmen who went into government, and their businesses had gone down. So I told God that I would leave my businesses if I took the cabinet position. Doing so meant taking both a personal financial risk and a personal risk of integrity. I would be giving up my income and my business reputation.

I had a severe struggle with God, trying to convince God that it wouldn't be responsible for me to step out of my businesses. I was sure this was an important "No." I argued, "Listen, God, I have really begun developing social responsibility in my businesses, and if I step away now, I'll put my employees at risk. They'll lose some of the stability they've begun to realize."

Then I remembered our business slogan, "Growing Together in Order to Serve," and I understood that this might be an opportunity to let that actually happen. In that moment, God showed me what a coward I was. I used a beautiful Christian slogan to work with my employees, but when it was my turn to become an employee, I wasn't interested at all.

God dealt pretty firmly with me concerning my businesses. He showed me, "Look, I gave you employees who are more capable than you are. You're almost a high-school dropout. I've given you employees with good brains. While you've been traveling around the world looking for foreign brands to work with, I've put increased human resources in front of you. This was not your merit. Your companies' value and success aren't because of you."

I suddenly thought, If I continue in my position as head of the company, how do I know these guys will stick with me? If they leave, I'll have nothing. They deserve to be upgraded. I had always preached to them, "Prepare for your successor." Now my turn had come, and I didn't have the courage to practice what I preached.

I consulted with my group of friends, some of whom were our executives in our businesses. They had a clear understanding of our country, its needs, and its overall situation. Their message to me was, "If you want to do something for the poor of the country, then you should do it." They understood the cost they would bear if I were to do this, so I was impressed that they were encouraging me to take the position. I got a promise of their moral support. But they agreed that things would not be easy.

Although the church community is very crucial to me, I didn't want to ask it for advice until I had cleared up some of my business involvements. Asking the church after I had consulted with others did not indicate that it was of lesser importance to me.

The pastor of our church was my brother, Holly. I asked him how I should get the advice of the congregation. We agreed that I would ask to meet with the board of elders. I invited them all to our house. For my local congregation, this was a new and not-so-easy a situation. The leaders had taken the traditional position of being basically critical about involvement in government. So this would be a fascinating meeting.

I was still looking for a "No," but I also wanted the truth. When we got together, I felt like I was in a meeting with diplomats and chancellors. We sort of danced around things, being very careful, too careful, in fact.

One leader whom I hold in very high esteem was outspoken against my accepting the post. He was very cautious about encouraging a positive answer; he was not at all convinced I should accept. The atmosphere was quite tense.

Our congregation had done some theological studying about Christians in politics, and also about how to reach consensus. So we had a bit of background for this moment.

There was another reason why this was not a totally foreign subject for us. The President's wife, Maria Gloria

Penayo Solaeche, was a member of our church's Spanish-speaking congregation. The board of elders who met at our home that evening oversaw both congregations—the German-speaking one, to which I belonged, and the Spanish-speaking one, to which Gloria had belonged for a number of years. But despite that, the board didn't feel cornered or squeezed by the First Lady's membership. Our discussion boiled down to this question: Which is more responsible for me—to say "Yes" or to say "No"?

The eight of us in the meeting didn't disagree so much as deliberate.

Is this an opportunity for service? This is an invitation to someone not affiliated with a political party or with the military. We can't give a blank endorsement for political activity, but maybe there are times that it's okay. Public service should always serve others and should not be entered for any other reason.

At the end of the evening, the group recommended that I accept. They wanted to see that good resources were contributed to the new government.

Not long after that, I had another encounter with God about what I should do. I remembered my grandfathers coming to Paraguay without anything and the Paraguayan people opening their arms to them. And the local people continued to be supportive and generous to the Mennonites who moved into Paraguay. Over time my people had gained considerable success, both socially and economically. I realized that God had not brought our immigrant people into Paraguay just so they could make a good living. I suddenly understood this clearly from God.

God had given me a strong home with good principles to grow up in. God had protected me from many wrong ways. I had gotten the best wife possible and, with her, a healthy family of our own. And I had spectacular business success, although I had been a poor student in my formal training. Suddenly, I also realized that what I had learned in seminars about leadership and working with people was important preparation for this challenge.

God wasn't asking me to sacrifice or make a specific contribution. God was giving me the privilege and the opportunity to offer back to the Paraguayan people some of the good that I had received, and some of the generosity and hospitality that my people had received. Suddenly I had a change of mood. The invitation to serve in government no longer felt like an obligation to avoid, but a privilege to return some of the good that had come to me from this country and its people.

This was an important turning point for me. But immediately I wondered, What happens if I fail? I was aware that I was taking a considerable risk. Bible reading and other reading helped me believe that it truly is better and more noble to try and fail, than not to try at all.

From then on, my mind was clear and I prepared to talk to the President. It had only been three weeks since the President asked me to walk out onto the lawn with him.

I began reading a lot in the Bible about David, Moses, and Nehemiah. I kept noticing that in their lives it was more important to be obedient than to rely on perfect training.

I made a deal with God. I said, “Okay, this is a privilege, but I want you to help me to be faithful. I want you to not permit me to abandon you at any moment in this process. I want you to help me stay close to you the entire time I’m in the government.” And that’s what I communicated to my church when I was asked to give my testimony. I said, “I don’t know if I will stay days, weeks, months, or years in the government. I am asking God that when I leave, I will have grown closer to him and more faithful to Jesus than I am today. That’s the most important part for me.”

And then I sat down at my computer and wrote a list of conditions and requests for the President. This, in summary, is what he would have to agree and commit to in order for me to do the job as well as I could:

1. God will continue to be my first and ultimate authority.
2. The well-being of the population will always guide and inform my decisions ahead of Party interests.
3. I need the liberty to choose my own team.
4. I will need access to the President and his personal counsel, since I don’t have political experience.

We set an evening to meet at the President's home. He and I went to one room; Gloria and Lucy to another room. I had my list along, and we went over the items point by point. I wanted to make sure he understood every one. I was prepared for him to tell me how impractical my requests were, or that he would try but couldn't promise to go along with all that I was asking.

When we finished reviewing the list the President said, "In addition to what you have asked, I give you my full personal and political support so that together we might have success." Later on I realized that I hadn't asked for this backup, but it was the most important thing of all. After he agreed unconditionally to do all that I asked, he said, "Well, Ernesto, let's pray to God about this."

President Nicanor Duarte (right) conferring with Ernst.

He started praying, and I was very impressed by his prayer. In fact, I could not pray at that point, so I thanked him, and we went to be with our wives. I didn't know him that well, but I learned that he does pray regularly.

The whole time I worked with the President, I felt his unconditional support to do whatever I thought I should do.

As I said, I didn't know Nicanor really well at that time. But I knew he was a politician, and I suspected that he did not have a clear picture of the economic details of the country. One of my conditions was that I would be free to run the economic affairs related to the Ministry of Industry and Commerce. Rumor had it that his invitation to me was just a short-term effort to broaden his political support, probably three to four months long. At the end of the calendar year, ministers traditionally changed.

Even if my time in office was likely to be short, I kept arguing with God that I was not prepared for the job. But I did notice in my reading that God called David when he was a young boy taking care of the sheep, and he called Nehemiah who was simply a waiter. God still had jobs for them—to lead God's people and to build the walls.

Still, I couldn't shake the question of whether I was really up to the job. But then I remembered that I was almost an outlaw, and that Lucy was the sum of all the social virtues one could hope for—and God gave her to me! I saw the same pattern in my business experience. I had become one of the most successful businessmen in the colonies under the age of 40. I was not unusually efficient, and other people had more training and experience than I had. In this whole struggle about whether I had the capacity for the job, I slowly came to believe that obedience to God was the reason I should act, rather than cause-and-effect results that I could measure.

Chapter 7

Why a Convinced Business Entrepreneur Reluctantly Joined the Government

I had grown up believing that we should pray for our governing authorities. Period. But now I had come face-to-face with a question. If we pray faithfully, and then those civil leaders discover capable people within the church and invite them to serve in public life, is it incoherent, even unfaithful, to refuse?

Reluctantly, I had agreed to join Nicanor's government. I assumed that one of my first tasks was to gather the experts for my team.

I've been successful in business, but I know my weaknesses well.

- I have little formal training.
- I have a short memory.
- I get dizzy when I fly.
- I can work intensively for only about an hour, and then I need a break.

But I have two strengths.

- I can develop a pretty clear vision for the future and then shape a strategic plan to realize it.
- I have the ability to form good working teams.

I was ready to move. I decided who the best guys were to invite, whose integrity I also trusted. And I made my appeals to them with Exodus 18:21 in my back pocket. Jethro, Moses' father-in-law, had observed Moses at the point of exhaustion. He gave him some advice: "Look for able men among all the people, men who fear God, are trustworthy, and hate dishonest gain. Set such men over the people as officers over thousands, hundreds, fifties, and tens."

That's when I met my first big frustration. I went to the best people I knew. I traveled thousands of miles, and I talked for hours and hours, trying to persuade them, but no one was willing to help me as Vice Minister. And I learned a lesson from God: It's not so important how big the dog is, but how willing the dog is to fight. In other words, it is more critical to find people with commitment than people with vast amounts of knowledge or extensive experience. A deep level of commitment to the poor and to those who are treated unjustly is greater than a head full of expertise.

I backed up and re-focused. I still knew nothing about the government's inner workings, so I needed adroitness there, *and* I wanted to choose people who cared about the needy.

At last, after a severe personal struggle as I moved from idealism to realism, I picked my two lead co-workers from within the Ministry of Industry and Commerce, from the environment in which I would work. That surprised people. Nicanor was elected on the platform of renewal. Everyone expected all of us to bring in new resources. These career public servants weren't expected to be chosen. But it turned out that they contributed very favorably to my work because I didn't need to train them. They could teach me, and so we were able to advance faster than other *Ministerios*, or departments.

Miriam Segovia was the current Vice Minister of Commerce. She had performed well and I re-affirmed her in that position. She was trusted by the people she worked with and was very honored to continue. Second, I needed a Vice Minister in the area of Industry. Jorge von Horoch had been the Director of the Technical Cabinet. He had refused corruption. In fact, he had not advanced further because of his integrity. When I invited him to serve as the Vice Minister of Industry, he didn't expect that at all. He quickly showed his deep commitment to the task and became my right-hand person. Eventually he went with me to the Ministry of Finance.

When I explained my vision for the Ministry of Industry and Commerce, Miriam and Jorge clearly shared it, committed themselves to it, and remained faithful to it.

The Ministry of Industry and Commerce has two main tasks: to encourage and foster national industry and commerce, and to elaborate the regulations for both industry and commerce. The Ministry is charged with fighting piracy, promoting development, and counseling companies.

I had a vision, and now I needed a plan. First, I did a diagnosis of the country's condition, trying to sum up simply what I found so that people could understand. Social upheaval was everywhere. The situation was essentially ungovernable. Corruption had infiltrated all areas of the economic system. Public and state employees were being paid months after their salaries were due, so they where highly uncertain and anxious. Desperate peasants were demonstrating their frustration by creating literal road blockades.

Outside creditors to the government were closing down our loans and financial credit. The government was late in making all kinds of payments, so construction projects had been slowed or stopped, pharmacy supplies for hospitals were at a standstill, and full deliveries of food for the army and for hospitals were not being delivered because the government could not make payments. We were living on "selective default"—choosing whom and how much to pay because we couldn't pay everyone.

There was no dialogue between the government and the business sector. The population in general was almost hopeless. The people had very little self-esteem and so had lost any belief about what they could achieve.

While I was soul-searching about whether or not to enter the government, I kept asking myself, What is government good for? I thought maybe my question was too simplistic; I just wasn't clear. I consulted within government and without, and almost no one was able to give me a good answer.

I did discover in the Bible that government is to seek the well-being of the people. As that settled on me, I wondered how to translate that idea into official language without being perceived as overly religious. As I organized the Industry and Commerce Ministry, I wanted a succinct phrase that could guide the department. "Political power should be good for all," embodied what I was thinking, but it didn't ring right. And then one day I found the catchy, graspable wordplay I was looking for—"Work for All."

Trabajo Para Todos. Everyone must make an effort so we can succeed together. The slogan plays two ways—Things will only work if everyone works. So how could the government foster that reality? I decided to focus on two things—recovering hope and self-esteem.

Once we admitted that our country needed intensive care, it became clear that our work would be a slow and complicated process. Where to start? We decided to set objective numbers that we wanted to achieve. First, we would try to create more jobs, more work opportunities. For that, we needed more money. There were two ways to generate more money. First, raise our exports so more money from the outside would come in. We set a goal as we took over in August '03 to double the country's exports during our government's five-year term. We would base our projections on Paraguay's export figures at the end of December, 2002.

People who heard our numbers thought we were crazy. But I was able to gather a team who was convinced we could do it, led by Victor Varela, an entrepreneur with a heart and vision geared toward exports. We shaped a National Plan of Export with the help of Paraguayan and outside professionals who put the details of the plan together. Part of the Export Plan was to improve our production of manufactured goods, not just raw, agricultural products. We wanted to improve our industrial sector. A Japanese agency had developed a plan called Chain of Production, which had been put aside by the previous Paraguayan government. We re-instituted it and used it to more than triple the export production of the country at any time in its history.

The Chain of Production called for a completely new approach, with the government coaching clusters of production. For example, it began with cattle ranchers, and included all who were involved in bringing beef to the grocery stores and restaurant tables, and it brought them together. The same thing happened in the sugar and textile industries. In less than two years about a dozen such clusters came together, including both private and public sectors. Each asked, "How can we export more?" Each agreed, "We must manufacture better to create more jobs and to distribute wealth more fully."

From my experience in business I believed it was essential that the private sector catch the vision and become the engine. The government could only coach.

Before the end of four years, we were able to meet our export goal. In 2006, Paraguay was honored as the country with the greatest increase of exports within all of Latin America. Our plan worked far better than I had dreamed. So our one strategy for bringing in more money was working.

The second way of generating more money, well-being, and jobs was to distribute the existing wealth more justly. We needed to strengthen the middle class and help the neediest segment of society. We had the international figures. Globally, Latin America has the worst equitable distribution of wealth. And Paraguay is one of the worst within Latin America. How to go against that?

Ernst (in center, wearing headsets for translation) in Washington, D.C. with a Congressional committee.

First, we had to formalize the economy by fighting and reducing black markets, tax evasion, and unregistered businesses. Most economic activity was undeclared; it happened outside the tax system. A significant part of Paraguayan economic transactions took place at the margin or outside the law. The great beneficiaries were high society and big businesses. The best way to correct that was to bring them *into* the system so they would operate *within* the law.

The Finance Minister, with whom I worked quite closely, prepared a series of reforms aimed significantly at improving the distribution of wealth: we put in place declarations of personal income, and we created tax laws. We were promoting new forms of tax collection; among others, a personal income tax and a tax on land holdings. The greater the amount of land held, the higher the percentage of tax. These two taxes were part of a larger fiscal law addressing the need for the country's economic turnaround. This was the vision we created for the "outside." Internally, we made four "planks":

1. *Development*: Our desired results are to have less poverty and more employment, human dignity, peace and social harmony, and efficient and transparent work. Externally, we made a strong public relations effort to promote this vision. (For example, why do people work in the department, and what are we up to?) Internally, we trained ourselves to think, Have I created a job opportunity for anyone today?

2. *Justice*: We will strive to have a just country in which everyone benefits from his/her own efforts.
3. *Cooperation*: Unity generates a sense of belonging. We will try to foster that, as well as togetherness. As much as possible, we will work to engage both the private and public sectors in cooperative development.
4. *We are each a role model and example*: You and I together are responsible for a Paraguay that is more competitive, trustworthy, and predictable.

Jorge von Horoch was my main colleague in the fight against piracy. During his term as Vice Minister, he was able to destroy stolen or fraudulent CDs (compact disks, which have traditionally been a huge black-market item in our country) that were worth millions of dollars. In fact, he was so thorough that Paraguay was no longer considered internationally to be a country that winked at piracy. Thanks to Jorge's efforts and those of his staff, the U.S. Congress invited us to share a report about our experiences in fighting piracy.

For me, Jorge is an example of how young people and young professionals with a high level of commitment to the well-being of the country can achieve an amazing impact and produce necessary changes.

One day just before Christmas, an official stepped into my office in the Ministry of Industry and Commerce. There was an unusual moment of tranquility, and so he asked if he could tell me a story. He wanted me to hear it from him and not from anyone else.

In Paraguay, it's common to send Christmas baskets with a card to one's friends in government to express gratitude for something in particular. He said that among the gifts he had received was a tea box with a Christmas card, which contained $5,000 (U.S.) in cash, from a woman in the industry sector. She was thanking him for support she had received.

This official explained that he found himself in a delicate situation. If he publicly denounced the gift, this influential woman would deny having given it. Furthermore, such a statement from him could severely harm his working relationship with the industry sector. If he kept the money, he would be guilty of an act of corruption.

This amount of money was equivalent to several months of his salary. By being open with me about this, he was exercising significant honesty and integrity.

My visitor had gotten an idea. He knew a Catholic priest who did excellent work caring for street children and heading a nonprofit organization which provided shelter for them. He had gone to this priest and asked him if he would be willing to accept a donation from a wealthy woman in favor of his work. Of course, the priest accepted gladly. Once everything was planned with the priest, he called the woman and invited her to accompany him to see an important project. They went together to visit the institution for street children. There they met with the priest and his staff. The government official introduced the woman as someone who cared a lot for poor children and who had given a significant gift to the work. And then he asked the priest to coordinate processing the donation legally. The woman was so touched that she was moved to tears. She had also understood the quiet lesson.

I had begun strong vision-building within the government and encouraged it also, along with my staff, in the private sector. I toured businesses and talked about what the Ministry of Industry and Commerce wanted to achieve. Slowly, together, we instituted "Work for All."

At the Brandenburg Gate in Berlin, with the Mayor of the city, gesturing to President Duarte. Ernst is the second to the left of the President.

Chapter 8

Attracting Good People

I quickly experienced the stress and tension of being in government. By nature I'm sober and tense; the President, on the other hand, is fun.

I don't like to fly, especially in helicopters. The President loves to fly, especially in helicopters! Soon after I took office with Industry and Commerce, the country celebrated its national holiday for industry. As part of my effort to engage the private sector in Paraguay's economic rehabilitation, the President and I decided to do a quick tour that would draw attention to our new emphasis. We took a day to fly—in a helicopter—to several industries to deliver pep talks. It was the first time I had done such a tour.

It was raining and windy. The President and I didn't know each other too well. When the helicopter took off,

I thought we were facing certain death. I was rethinking my life. I was sweating and about to throw up.

The President was in a good mood. The helicopter hit a vacuum and dropped in a free-fall. The President embraced me and said, "Ernst, don't worry. You'll leave a very rich widow and she'll have many suitors. I want you to know that my wife won't be in such good shape. But we shouldn't worry. Lucy is rich and Gloria has five children, so together they'll be okay!" I said nothing, dedicated to prayer that we'd survive somehow.

I was catching on that a good measure of humor could be very helpful. The President was a genius at using humor in quite difficult situations. I would need his example when I was being publicly observed, and as I assembled my team off-stage.

Ernst (left) and the President leave a meeting in Asunción.

I was clear about my goal for myself and for the Ministry of Industry and Commerce staff. "We must generate job opportunities for all, and I will equip you to do this," I told my staff. "Your responsibility is to create an atmosphere of job opportunities and to convince the people that there are enough jobs for everyone. I'm responsible to help you succeed at this."

I tried to do strong motivational work with them. I said, "You know how to play the game. You will make the score. I will be your coach, your technical director." A related goal I had was to talk to the press as little as possible. My strategy from the start was that staff should own the success and then communicate the success. After all, they were the technicians and could give better answers than I could. I needed them to bring about "Work for All," along with our four planks and specific numerical goals. I believed that the right staff, appropriately motivated, could do the job of the department.

So who were the ideal staff people? First, I knew it was essential that I communicate clearly about what staff should expect from me. The political and economic environment was insecure, unstable, and in turmoil. I had to begin shaping the minds and attitudes of the state employees who would work for me, and of the private sector who had little reason to be loyal to me. I wanted them all to know that I intended to generate a consensus on a shared vision and build commitment to it. Within the Paraguayan cultural tradition this was a little unusual. Generally, the tradition has been to build loyalty to a person. But my plan was well received. I appealed especially to staff, and to business leaders at the executive level, to make our priority the well-being of the whole population.

Jesus had called his disciples with a straightforward statement: "I will make you fishers of men." My goal was to be as direct with "Work for All." The phrase was simple and easy to understand. It did put me on the spot because people could measure me against the slogan and see if I was living up to it, if I was seriously insisting on it. Latin America's experience with years of military dictatorships has created an atmosphere which assumes that what the leader wants is law for the rest of the population. I had to urgently correct this, to redirect popular thinking to a larger vision.

I began by interviewing all leaders within the department to see if they'd stay with me. They prepared well for these exchanges. I checked them out on two levels—their commitment and their competence.

First, I asked them to tell me about their families—their marriages, parents, children. I was trying to measure their commitment to others. Most of them had prepared a fantastic presentation about their competencies. I usually didn't spend much time on that part. Rumors passed through the department about this strange way of being interviewed!

Second, I was interested in their attitude toward money. This was obviously of special concern because of the possibility for corruption in a government position. I asked provocative questions: "What do you want to own in 10 years?" "What would you like to be in 10 years?" I had asked similar questions in my companies when I hired people who were aware of the businesses' prosperity. But I was concerned about more than money in my questions. What was their attitude toward leisure, wine, the use of time? I wanted to identify what they did with their free time; for example, were they party-goers?

I had asked for their CVs ahead of time, before the interviews. I wanted the interviews to be personal, informal, and relaxed. I tried to sense how these persons would treat others.

Most of the staff entered my office in an attitude of crisis; the interviews were quite unusual. These people had degrees and long-standing careers. But I wanted them to understand that that wasn't something to fall back on. I was concerned with the kind of people they were. A government position was considered a secure job, and one in which they could not be easily displaced. I had intentionally unsettled them and made them feel insecure. I wanted to observe their characters.

Finally, I explored their attitudes toward God. I knew most were Catholic, but I wanted to discover if they had a personal relationship with God. My questions were pretty challenging: "What do you believe?" "What will happen if you die tomorrow?" "Why are you here?" Many would answer, "I'm this; I'm that." I said, "I'm not interested in *what* you are, but your purpose for being here."

Most staff couldn't say why they worked for the Ministry of Industry and Commerce. I believe that my interviews began to stir some new thinking within many of them. My vision was simple—we were there for the people of Paraguay. Most importantly, I tried constantly to measure myself so I could be a model.

In my strategy for forming public servants, the personal commitment of the staff was most important, was Number One, and each staff member's individual capacity was right beside that. But I had three equally as essential guiding principles for myself. First, people must feel attracted to my leadership. I had to demonstrate that I wanted the best for them as we worked at our common task. This included the way I would support them in times of crisis. How I would handle a situation if our working relationship came to an end. How I would support them and secure their futures if we needed to part ways because of loyalty questions.

Second, I had to be committed to their best interests, or they would have no enduring reason to stay. I would keep them in top condition. I would help them renew themselves and maintain themselves well while working for the ministry. Staff members would have a good future in the institution even after I was gone.

I had a well established plan for refreshing the first circle of leaders. They would attend seminars, go on retreats, read books which I suggested so we could talk about them. Jesus had said, "I will make you…." That meant to me that a leader would take responsibility for the growth and preparation of the people who worked with him.

Third, I would do what was best for them so that they would want to stay in the Ministry. Jesus said that bread alone does not sustain a human being. A salary raise isn't everything. I had to understand the needs of each person who worked with me and develop a plan about how to help him/her in each area of life. To a young guy about to get married, money is important. But he needs to learn how to spend money. A co-worker who is more established financially may be looking for social connections, so I must free him to develop good social activities. As a signal that that's important, I might offer him a recreational area to use for his self-fulfillment.

In Paraguay it's hard to retain good people in their jobs. Developing trust is critical. I wanted an atmosphere in which an employee would tell me what other employment offers he was getting. I could consider matching those so he would feel motivated to stay and not switch.

I had been invited to lead the Ministry of Industry and Commerce because the country was in an economic crisis. I was gathering a team to meet concrete growth goals. I intended to succeed at that, but also at being a leader in Jesus' style. My natural style is getting to simple answers! But I believe absolutely that a good leader embodies and practices integrity. If Jesus hadn't had integrity, his total work would have lacked credibility.

You don't just decide to have integrity. I committed myself to striving honestly for it and to surrounding myself with people who also wanted to have integrity. That was crucial for me. I knew I must be willing to forgive. But I was aware, too, that I would have to check whether after repentance a person demonstrated real integrity and a wish to improve and change.

I remembered that when Jesus was putting his team together, he didn't analyze who had the best public profile. He walked around the Sea of Galilee and looked for simple people with a high commitment to the cause. They didn't have to have a high level of knowledge, but they needed a high level of commitment to the vision. Another thing I learned from Jesus was that he was able to communicate his ideas very simply. People will follow a simply stated, convincing vision, especially if the leader lives it.

Ernst greeting President of Germany
Horst Koehler and Mrs. Koehler.

"I had the privilege of sitting at the same table at dinner with the Koehlers. President Koehler, in conversation with Nicanor and the rest of us at the table, said, 'The time has come for political leaders to speak with clarity, and not use "diplomatic" language. Otherwise, the citizens don't know what the issues are because of our "political makeup."' I was impressed by his courage."

I was beginning a process of building loyalty. The more lobbying a staff asked others to do on his/her behalf, the further down my list they moved. The most "secure" began to catch on.

Early on I was confronted with the issue of salaries, which were very low. I told the staff I agreed that they were underpaid, and I wanted them to earn more. But I also said that I needed them to show to the public that Industry and Commerce was a well functioning Ministry. The people would have to feel it. Once that happened, I could make significant efforts to increase their salaries. But I knew that that was only one part of my job. I wanted this staff to recover a sense of dignity from being in public service, to believe that their work contributed to the well-being of the whole country. Industry and Commerce notoriously had the worst infrastructure of all the Ministries.

I told the President, "These people are working in rat-like conditions." We began to look for a new building immediately. The government had acquired a former bank building, and we were able to move the department into it. It turned out to be a great location.

Many on the staff had been receiving bribes and informal "pay." I restructured the way the department had worked, where money flowed informally to and from the "untouchables" who had been tenured into high positions. I moved different people into these posts, people who weren't trapped in the old practices.

We still had two big problems: salaries, and a failing sense of dignity within the department.

I increased the budget several times to improve the functioning of the Ministry. I met great resistance when I tried to bring in computer-programming in order to systemize payments, because that dramatically diminished possibilities for under-the-table dealings. Industry and Commerce was known to be a department with a lot of corruption. But the President ordered us not to look back and pursue those who had done wrong, but to look forward. The public was seeing some improvements and was beginning to support our moves. And I was gaining a lot of support from private businesspeople.

I stayed close to a group of about 50 persons whom we tried to relocate because we had some doubts about their performances in the Ministry. I talked with them and especially listened to them, encouraging them to change their way of doing things. They told me, "Minister, we dance to the music our leader is making. We will dance to your music." I realized the low level of character they had, and I was saddened by it. They needed help. We tried to create new opportunities for them where they wouldn't be as close to money.

We tried to formalize procedures that I hope will survive this president, but that can't be assured. I had this concern from the first day as I tried to install procedures for good government. And we tried hard to treat the private sector well. Hopefully, if old practices return later, private businesses will object.

For example, previously a company had to go through 17 registration steps in order to be able to export product. In those 17 steps, there were numerous possibilities for corruption. Today this registering can be done in one place. It's all computerized. The registration certification is ready within 48 hours. In fact, today we have one of the best systems in Latin America for open and transparent government purchasing.

Twenty-three months after I took office, the Ministry of Industry and Commerce was analyzed to be one of the best functioning government departments. But it was never a smooth ride.

Chapter 9

Finding My Way

I had a strict rule: "We will not lie to anyone and we won't nurture false expectations." If we generated false expectations, we'd be expected to do even more than we were attempting. We wouldn't tolerate that. We couldn't do it. It was hard enough to do what we promised.

When I stepped into the office of Industry and Commerce, I wanted to increase the production of ethanol to create more jobs. We mixed 12 percent ethanol to 88 percent gasoline in fuel at that point. We were authorized to raise ethanol to 20 percent and reduce gasoline to 80 percent. I called together all ethanol producers to discuss how we could further develop this market. Paraguay imports all its gasoline, but we have a good potential to increase domestic production of ethanol. After meeting with ethanol producers, I called together gas-station owners and discussed with them how to increase the ethanol market.

A federal regulation gave the Minister of Industry and Commerce the power to set the percentage of ethanol to gasoline in fuel. With a lot of enthusiasm we were able to raise production of ethanol and the gradual incorporation of higher percentages in the fuel mixture within a relatively short period. We called a big press conference to announce job creation as a result. After a couple of months we were at 14 percent, and then at 16 percent.

Then the sugar cane/ethanol production season was over, and we faced a shortage of ethanol. The oil producers asked that I lower the ethanol percentage. It didn't make sense to me. I put the decree aside and didn't sign it. The oil producers became dramatic. I asked the oil technicians, "Why should I sign the law allowing the ethanol percentage to drop?" Their explanations didn't make sense, and I didn't believe what they said. On the other hand, some technicians were not in favor of dropping the ethanol percentage. So in a simple but clear way I asked the group who defended the dropping percentage, "Who will benefit if the price of ethanol rises?"

They said what I knew. If prices rise, small sugar-cane producers benefit. The price of ethanol will go up and up. Strong public debate developed about why the Minister wouldn't sign the resolution permitting a lower percentage of ethanol. One day I read in a newspaper, "The resolution is on the desk of the Minister and has been for a while [which was true], but he is not willing to sign!" Clearly I had touched a very sensitive and powerful nerve in the social-economic system.

I knew that we might reach a real shortage of ethanol, but lowering the price and the percentage again would have a harsh effect on producers. I made the subject the focus of my personal prayers. I consulted with my most intimate co-workers. We wanted to reach a decision together about what was best for most of the people. Some technicians within the Ministry defended the interests of the fuel and gas-station lobbies. They told me, "Mr. Minister, we do not have enough ethanol to make it 18 percent of the mixture. You have to do something urgently!" My concern was more for the poor, in this case the producers of sugar cane. But if there was a *true* shortage of ethanol, I was facing more complications.

I decided to sign a resolution which stated that the proportion of ethanol "will be up to 18 percent." This meant that the demand would continue to exist, but if it couldn't be met, the law was not being violated.

I released a statement saying that as soon as production is able, we will raise the proportion of ethanol to 20 percent, and even up to 24 percent when national production is able to meet that proportion. That statement allowed the suppliers to increase their supply with security. I repeated the slogan, "Work for All," and stated that I was definitely on the side of the ethanol producers.

The stand-off brought two results. I made some powerful enemies. And in the space of four years, we were able to increase production of ethanol to at least four times the amount produced when Nicanor took office (for example, from 1 liter to more than 4 liters).

There's no doubt that the cost of defending the needy from within the Ministry of Industry and Commerce is high, but whoever has the courage to do that will soon see encouraging results. I want to acknowledge that some gas-station owners understood the situation perfectly and supported my decision.

Ernst greeting Hugo Chavez, President of Venezuela.

Today, four years later, and no longer holding public office, I see with satisfaction that the situation with ethanol has matured enormously in all sectors. Production is consolidated. There is a general consensus to use renewable oil energies and bio-fuel. Thanks to this consensus, the government recently approved a decree which guarantees duty-free import for vehicles with a full-flex capacity. These vehicles have a technology which allows their motors to adapt and use gas, ethanol, or any mixture of both. This decree guarantees the possibility of increasing the production of ethanol and a better future for sugar-cane producers across the country.

Before entering government I tried to learn about communication, reporters, newspapers, TV. Since the President-Elect had been a journalist, I approached him and told him how little I knew. I asked him to teach me. I was ready to write down all of his advice. But he gave me just one sentence, and I remember it vividly: "If you make shit, flush it down right away." I expected more help, but he thought that was enough. He wanted me to know that I'd make mistakes, but that I'd have to just keep going.

I went to a few more professionals and asked their advice. One explained how communication works. "If a headline reads 'Dog Bites Man,' that's not news. But changing two words makes a great story and breaking news: 'Man Bites Dog.'" With that he showed me that papers need to sell, and so they need to offer spectacular news, independent of what really happened. Another politician, leader of the Colorado Party and Minister, told me, "No flies can get into a closed mouth." I tried to stick to these lessons from the President and his friends. The more examples I got, the better I understood the wisdom of their counsel.

An official visit of Paraguayan officials to France; former French President Jacques Chirac is in the right foreground. Ernst is above and to his left.

"What amazed me about President Chirac, considering his age and experience, was how keenly interested he was in Nicanor's opinion about what was going in Paraguay—which was of little consequence to France. An old seasoned political leader with global influence took a lot more time than was on the agenda to encourage and mentor a young Latin American leader in his first term. He listened carefully to Nicanor as he answered Chirac's questions about what was happening in Latin America.

"I learned how important it is for a leader of that stature to display interest toward a country which is developing and towards a young leader. Nicanor remembers this as one of his most important meetings ever with a world leader.

"The French are highly regarded in Latin America. Chirac even helped Nicanor into his car at the end of the meeting. Chirac's human side was very impressive."

In a prestigious public job, you attract lots of enemies and people eager to criticize your work, including the press who are gifted at highlighting your mistakes. I read somewhere that if you persecute the poisonous snake that has been biting you, the only thing you'll achieve is having the poison spread throughout your body. You should extract the poison entirely from your organism as soon as possible.

When I received harsh attacks, and my frustration level grew and I wondered how I could harm these people, I realized that the snake bite had begun poisoning me. I started looking for ways to get rid of the poison. I developed a strategy for dealing with my anger. I began writing letters to the offending persons which I knew I wouldn't send. The exercise helped me immensely. I still do it from time to time!

I needed to staff Industry and Commerce with technicians and professionals. But I also needed another kind of resource around me so I wouldn't lose my way in the day-to-day crush. I needed help to keep my vision vividly in view.

In my businesses, and now in government, I liked to have people from society's margins on my staff. It is easy for me to identify with them. Their level of commitment is unusual, often far higher than the saints of the Lord and the well-prepared people. My driver, who later became Lucy's driver and is our grill meister, is a former prisoner. In my businesses and other involvements I have had co-workers who have been in prison. They see me in my public—and my private—moments. They are helpful in calming me down when I am about to explode, because they have learned to forgive. They have considerable deficits and have made many mistakes, but what they have come through, and the commitments they have made as a result, are very helpful to me. I confide in them. I am loyal to them and I consult with them.

I developed a high degree of confidence with my first level of co-workers, and I was committed to protecting their public dignity. Occasionally I slipped.

One guy could annoy me, and once when he especially upset me, I criticized him publicly. A group of us were in Belgium with the President, and at our next stop in Paris, this assistant was, as always, to reserve a room in the hotel for me beside the President's room. The only thing he came up with was a poor room in a different hotel. The whole trip was poorly planned, although that was not this guy's fault. Anyway, I was highly frustrated, and, unfortunately for him, he happened to be the only person in front of me. I gave him two options, loud enough for everyone nearby to hear: "Either you get me the right hotel room in Paris, or I hang you in a public square."

My assistant got the message, and the next time I got a *better* room than the President, which I discovered when the President came to my room for meetings! After my assistant had outdone himself, he came to me and said, "Don't threaten me again in public." He was newlywed and tended to be more preoccupied with satisfying the wishes of his new wife than of our mission. I recommended that he not confuse my instructions with those of his wife! But I was reminded to be respectful of everyone, no matter how frustrated I was.

If I was truly to influence my staff and my department, they would follow my lead because they respected me, and I them. Not because they were expected to or because I was authoritarian and insisted on it. I became more alert about my behavior and theirs. Was I showing them true respect—and receiving their authentic respect?

Chapter 10

Keeping One Foot in the Church – and in Prison

Our congregation in center-city Asunción has an active prison ministry. I got involved with it about 14 years ago, along with other members, including several other businessmen. I served on the church's prison-ministry committee, although I wasn't a very committed member. But in that capacity, I learned to know Felix Duarte. He went to prison some 25 years ago because he killed a person.

Felix has leadership capacity. He is a man of integrity, but there was a moment in his past when he lost self-control. On top of that, he had friends who were a bad influence, and he was drawn into an enormously complicated situation. I was deeply moved by the man as I learned to know him. I knew I was capable of committing the same crime he had.

Listening to Felix's story, I made a commitment to do something serious in our prison ministry. I wanted the ministry to belong to the congregation because I believed it could have a redemptive effect on our church. I tried to get more people involved. And I agreed to serve as president of the ministry, which I've done now for 12 years. It has been one of the few honorary positions I continued in while I was Minister of Industry and Commerce and Minister of Finance. It became an essential way for me to keep a church involvement during my time in government.

My ongoing contact with prisoners and ex-convicts has shaped me significantly. I am constantly reminded that leaders can make mistakes in pressured moments. Felix's life was forever changed by his impulsive act. But through repentance and redemption by God's mercy, he became a renewed person, thankful to God for what he has received and committed to helping our church be more effective in its work with prisoners.

When Felix had done his time and was released from prison, he tried to integrate into our church. The church was expecting him to be a "Mennonite," with the traditional habits and disciplines practiced by many of our members, but he would never fit that style. Some people almost stopped supporting him, but fortunately there was no break between him and the congregation. Today, he's one of the most important persons in our prison work, leading a pastoral ministry of restoration and rehabilitation.

Recently, in addition to the many reforms we helped to put in place years ago, we have constructed a new building within the prison where wives can come and even spend the night with their husbands in an atmosphere of dignity and privacy. It was a little hard for our congregation to accept and support this idea, but the building and program are well constructed and well administered. The building includes an office and an industrial shop, since one of the goals we have for the inmates is zero laziness.

We have also built a church with a baptismal pool within the penitentiary, and we have baptized more than 860 persons; in fact, more than the number of members in our congregation. At this moment we have 10 people employed full-time in the prison ministry. More than 700 prisoners are fully registered in our discovery Bible study. And we've been invited by the prison administration to extend our ministry by offering basic education courses, as well as technical and leadership trainings. Most recently we have reached an agreement with a local college to offer the study of law through the Internet.

It has been important for me to stay involved in the prison ministry because it helps me to be continually grateful for all the opportunities I've had. I've made sure that Felix has the financial support of the congregation so he can continue to minister in the prisons since his release. Our congregation's ministry has been recognized as significant by the society in general. Visitors to the penitentiary are often shown the *Iglesia Libertad*, the church inside the prison, and other sections of the buildings which were funded by our congregation. But about three months ago a prisoner committed suicide in one of these sectors. We were reminded that we are one small part of a desolate system of justice.

One of the principles of our ministry is that we will not intervene in the administration of justice to the prisoners. We operate our programs separately. Nor do we lobby before a judge. Trying to help prisoners spiritually is a challenge for many in our home church who are used to things being very clear. This is a very confusing world. One prisoner who was supposedly converted asked to talk with me. He had three wives, and now he was in love with a fourth woman. He asked me what he should do. I suggested he speak with a pastor. The standard Mennonite recipe doesn't function in such circumstances. We never tell the prisoners to stop smoking or drinking. But we accompany them until they get to that place themselves, inspired by the Bible studies they're participating in and the environment of support which we offer. People slowly come to these conclusions themselves, but in the meantime, they may be smoking during Bible study.

We have employed ex-convicts in our companies for years, and I have strongly encouraged other businesses to do this. Today a group of companies whose leaders are members of our congregation have a commitment to employ ex-convicts. This requires considerable courage and intention because it means exposing your systems to a person with significant problems. But this is the way social reintegration happens. We may feel our principles and our security are put at risk, but all of us must be involved, either actively or supportively. As Felix says, "No one leaves the prison as the same person who entered. He leaves either better or worse. The outcome on the outside is directly related to whether or not he has someone who will help him, and if he wants to be helped."

When I entered the government I employed a homicide ex-con as Lucy's driver. He had killed in order to protect a friend. He wanted to protect and not kill. Today he's a Christian. The man is loyal and reliable, but his past so shocked my official security that they decided to keep an extra eye on him. So Lucy's driver witnessed to them! Today we have theological students in the Mennonite seminaries in Paraguay who are ex-convicts.

Working with prisoners has transformed me considerably and helped me to live more conscientiously. Society judges many prisoners wrongly, and I include myself in that. I found people in prison who are much better than I am. They made a mistake in a bad moment, often because of stress or provocation, usually in just two or three minutes of their lives. And then they are put in prison, cut off from society. Whenever I visit there, I thank God that I am still free.

I have learned how careful I have to be not to judge people or to put them aside. When I talk to prisoners, I'm not talking to "lower" people. Often, they're superior to me, like my very close friend Felix, whom I consider better than myself. Our society has much more responsibility to prisoners than we're willing to admit.

In May, 2005, Nicanor asked me to leave the Ministry of Industry and Commerce and become Minister of Finance. The job included overseeing the whole national budget and more then 200,000 employees. I was scared. After church I called the Board of Elders together and said, "I'm not able to do this, and it will go badly unless God makes a miracle." I will never forget that it was my ex-con friend, a murderer, who helped me answer President Duarte's startling new question. "Ernst, remember that before you sat on the Finance Ministry, God sat there."

Ernst signs the official document, certifying that he is the Minister of Industry and Commerce for the government of Paraguay. President Nicanor Duarte sits second from left.

Chapter 11

Behaving Well, but Communicating Poorly

If entering government was one of the three biggest risks I took in my life, the second biggest had to be moving from the Ministry of Industry and Commerce to the Ministry of Finance.

I had had my share of crises in Industry and Commerce, but 21 months later I had brought the department well under control. We began harvesting what we had been planting.

It was not my goal to move on to another ministry. My gifts and my experience fit with promoting commerce, industry, and work, all with a positive agenda. The Finance Ministry, by far the most challenging Ministry since it defines the economy of the country and provides the means for the national budget, was led by Dr. Dionisio Borda. He was a professional with a solid background that prepared him well for the task. With a firm hand, he changed the way in which much needed reforms could take place. Together with his team of experienced co-workers, they had achieved extraordinary results by implementing fiscal and economic reform. For example, tax collection was increasing. Nevertheless, Dr. Borda decided to resign, and so the cabinet had a critical vacancy.

After some long and dark night-time sessions, the President had persuaded me to become Minister of Finance, even though I had not wanted this responsibility. Immediately I realized that I had a double challenge. On one hand, I wanted to give the existing team security and motivate them to continue with their good work. I never liked the idea that a new leader had to despise all that had been done previously. I believed with equal conviction that it was necessary to strengthen what had been done well and to correct the deficiencies. Fortunately, most of the good team at the Finance Ministry was willing to stay and work along with me.

On the other hand, my second challenge was to stop any false expectations from the business sector, which always wanted to pay fewer taxes. Since I came from business, they expected me to have a less firm hand, which of course would not benefit the poor majority and unemployed in our country. From the first day on I had to give a clear signal. In my first press conference as Finance Minister, I told them that they had a loyal ally in the Ministry and that we were open to dialogue about any topic—with the sole exception of tax reductions. On top of that, I gave precise instructions that no one in the whole Ministry was permitted to talk about the reduction or exemption of taxes. I must say that my business colleagues accepted this directive with great maturity.

I needed to move quickly and decisively. Within the few first months, we got a law passed implementing some fiscal and tax reform. The law allowed gradual reductions in taxes from 30 percent to 10 percent for businesses—on the condition that a 10 percent *personal* income tax would be enacted on people with higher incomes. This affected less than one percent of the population and only the most wealthy.

However, Parliament had the power to postpone implementation of the law and was studying the possibility of doing that. And then began a big debate in the press about the personal income tax. The President was getting pressure from his party and from Parliament to kill the idea. Although only the elite would be affected, our adversaries were able to install a very negative attitude toward the proposed law in the press and among all involved. A very vigorous public debate raged in the papers, on radio, and on TV. We were losing the battle.

One day the President asked me to stop at his office at home at 5:00 p.m. This was the time of day when the President sometimes dealt with his least favorite situations. When I got to his office a Party chapter leader was there. The President's Party—the Red, or Colorado, Party—has more than 1,000 different chapters, each with a local leader. This was one of those guys. I learned a lot from him about how politicians think and work. One of the richest and most important Senators from the Red Party arrived at the same time as I did. The President stepped out and welcomed the Senator, a very influential and famous businessman who was about 70 years old. The President embraced him fervently.

The President said, "I'm sure you've come to talk with me about the personal income tax. Well, the Finance Minister has just arrived, and since I don't understand this technical law very well, I'll let the two of you alone, and I'll meet with the lower party boss."

I said to the Senator. "I'm so glad for this opportunity to talk with you and to talk quietly and privately." He had already come out against the law publicly. He began to play along and say how important the law is, what an important social priority it is. He went on and on, talking about how he would love the pleasure of paying income tax because it's only fair, and how Paraguay is one of only two nations in South America without a personal income tax, which is absolutely necessary for social justice. He explained the virtues of the law better than I could have.

I was very surprised. This was unexpected. I replied, "I'm very impressed by your vision for giving the needs of the poor such a strong priority. I'm so glad for your support." Then I remembered what a friend had said: "Ernst, what counts in Parliament are the votes, not the speeches."

I said, "Most Excellent Mr. Senator, I congratulate you for your patriotic vision. I understand that we can count on your vote in Parliament." He looked at me as intently as when he was extolling the tax law's virtues and said, "No." I needed to exercise my self-control. I asked sympathetically, "Can you help me understand?!"

He said, "I'm a political animal. My aim is to be reelected. You have failed terribly to convince the public that this is an essential law. And I must vote for what the people want. I must go with the voters." He went on, "It's your turn to make a strong campaign to the public that the law is needed. When you've convinced the public to support it, you have my vote."

The President was taking a lot of time in the other room with the party leader. Finally he came out and said, "I'm sure you've resolved this." I went into his office, I told him what I had learned, and we quickly planned a strong campaign to persuade the people and the officials to support our position. But it was too late. We lost that battle. Parliament postponed implementing the law, and it hasn't yet acted to put it to work.

I had gotten the message. In government, it isn't enough to have all the good reasons on your side. You must make them legitimate to the people. In fact, convincing and communicating may be more primary at times than being on the right side of an issue. Then, when legitimization happens, it is more powerful because the people have become convinced it's the way to go. All of this made me think a lot. Had my performance been poor? I started to blame myself. And I found myself thinking about the example of Jesus.

Just three days before the crucifixion, the people proclaimed Jesus to be their king. I was touched profoundly by how on Palm Sunday, Jesus entered Jerusalem as king, with the people convinced and full of hope.

But that wasn't the pleasure of the elite political religious leaders, and they were able to change the mood of the people within three days. Once public opinion was manipulated by perverse leaders, those in political authority found themselves forced to crucify Jesus. Pilate found no violation of the law; Herod didn't have the legal tools to prohibit Jesus' execution. Both Pilate and Herod knew that what they did was not just, but finally they did it because of the popular legitimization of something incorrect.

I had learned that being right and having the best intentions is just a very small part in the process of change that you want to bring about in a country. The real challenge is to help the people believe in what you think ought to be done, what you consider to be correct, what expresses your good intentions.

I would need to recall these lessons a few more times. In December, 2005, the President was running for reelection as Chairman of his party. Things were hot. Parliament had approved a national budget that was inflated. We wouldn't have the necessary finances to do what it called for. I gathered my Vice Ministers and team. I told them, "We will end this year with a surplus, because we will spend less than our income." They said, "We have a Parliamentary-approved budget calling for a deficit of 1.6 percent of the GNP. The President is in a crucial year for his political future. The only way to stop spending and to balance the budget is with a tough, aggressive Presidential decree. And he won't issue one at this time."

I instructed them to write the decree that we needed as soon as possible. I called for a prohibition on hiring new employees for the next four months, until the elections were over. There would be no buying of vehicles except for ambulances and police security. And I put some other unpopular cost-saving measures in place.

The Vice Ministers with their teams worked hard late into the night, preparing the text of the decree. I also asked them to put together a PowerPoint presentation that would translate our message into political language. I got everything together that the President would need and then asked for an audience with him. I told him that I understood his current situation, but that the country needed his decree to balance the budget. He was sitting in his big chair.

"Don't worry, Ernst," he said. "Get this decree going. I will sign it." I said, "Thank you, Mr. President, but I need more." "What more can I give you?" his eyes asked, as he looked at me with a face that expressed more than a thousand words. "Isn't that enough?" I asked for a meeting of the cabinet so I could explain the decree to them with him present. I knew that such a decree was in a gray legal zone, and we needed the strong backup of the whole cabinet in this critical moment. We had to present a united front as an Administration. Several Ministers would be very critical. They needed to be popular at that time because they were facing re-election.

The President set the meeting for two days later. The President had a way of making us Ministers suffer so we'd integrate our agendas a little more and deal with each other, while he dedicated himself to things that apparently were more important! It was a hard two days for me.

My custom was to give an introduction, and then have my Vice Minister Miguel Gomez make the main presentation. He could explain complex things in a simple manner.

The President entered. He turned the meeting over to me. I needed to present the request so I was formal, calm, soft-of-voice. There were about 20 people in the room. I thanked them for their cooperation. I was responsible for gathering money; these cabinet ministers spent it. I had to loosen them up, relax them, so that I could get to the deeper parts of their hearts because we collaborated a lot together. But soon the President interrupted my strategic work and said, "Ernst is trying to butter you up in order to get his knife into you. This is bullshit. Give them the heavy message." But what I said, I really meant. These colleagues deserved recognition and respect for their efforts.

I said, "My Vice Minister will now present the decree." So Miguel went through it point-by-point. Some of the Ministers were in shock. The President was catching on to several of the details with more clarity. I was shaking; I didn't know where to hide. The others were loading their artillery. I looked at the President to see what was going on. I saw that his face was not exactly peaceful, and I prayed to God to deliver me.

Ernst addressing officials at the Presidential palace in Asunción, Paraguay. (President Duarte sits at the far left.)

The President said, "This is exactly what I wanted to see." He appeared to grasp what the rest of the cabinet was absorbing. "Whoever isn't willing to accept this, take a sheet of paper and write your resignation. If irresponsible public spending is needed for me to stay in power, I am not interested in being President." Then he asked, "Any questions?"

Only one cabinet minister had a timid question, and it was followed by a debate about its insignificance. The President paused and gave everyone in the room a chance to object to his decree, but with a warning—"If you do, you'll be replaced immediately. I ask for your support, and this is what our nation needs."

This decree opened a way for a new professionalism and seriousness in public spending. It also sent a clear message to cabinet Ministers to operate in a forthright way.

The only condition the President asked for that day was that the Ministry of Education should be permitted to continue hiring teachers so that the country's educational program wasn't harmed. A new school year was just starting. I became convinced that our government, and especially the President, was of one mind regarding the needs of our country. The people of Paraguay could not conceive that their government would think of public needs ahead of private interests.

I, along with my team, became much more loyal to the rest of the cabinet after this. We had a renewed commitment to work together for the betterment of the country. After that meeting I felt strong support and the commitment of the whole government to do what was right for the people. In that moment, the President and cabinet were willing to pay the price, take risks, and give up benefits in order to strengthen our economy and bring better conditions for the poor.

Chapter 12

Staying Sane

I knew it from experience—leaders tend to make poorer decisions when they're under stress. So I figured out several ways to safeguard myself and to keep from aggravating my natural weaknesses.

I have a simple principle I aim to practice: In order to understand the newspapers I have to read the Bible. That combination doesn't answer all the questions, but it has kept me grounded and focused on the right things.

I get up early. At 6:30, Lucy prepares breakfast for me, and I eat it in the study at home. Then I do my reading and plan the day until 7:45. When I was in government I would be in my public office by 8:00 a.m. Most of my colleagues listened to the radio during their drives to the office. My first instruction to my chauffeur was, "Never turn on the radio in the car."

I made a lot of phone calls to co-workers in the car on the way to the office, giving them instructions for the day, clarifying what was important. I usually stayed in the office until 2:00 p.m. Sometimes I went home for lunch after that, and to rest a little bit. If possible, I walked for several hours in the afternoon out in nature.

Most of the time while I was walking I was on the phone. I didn't answer the phone while I was in the office, but my efficient office assistant, Rachel, registered my incoming calls. I'd answer them during my afternoon walks. I was usually on the phone in the afternoon for two to four hours. And I was often able to achieve more in those conversations than I did in all the meetings I attended. I asked for counsel and coordinated work to be done in the Ministry.

The phone calls allowed me to listen to many people and to offer encouragement during those quiet moments. I prepared for meetings with key players, and I found that if I allowed time, they would often spill their frustrations out in the phone calls, rather than in larger meetings. This approach gave me the advantage of getting closer to many people with whom I worked regularly—coaching, mentoring, listening.

I decided, whenever possible, not to accept any glittering, fashionable invitations to dinners or meetings in the evenings. On nearly every Thursday I would receive three invitations for events throughout the weekend. I turned down almost all of them for two reasons: I needed time to evaluate, reflect, and be alone. And at those events I would be asked for favors or be pressured to do certain things. I had brilliant Vice Presidents, and I asked them to take turns representing me at those occasions. Some enjoyed doing that; some didn't!

The President loved to call his Ministers starting at 5:00 in the morning, when he began doing business at his home. He very much enjoyed finding some of his Ministers still sleepy at that hour. He would say, "That's the way it is. You're sleeping while I am working!" At 7:00 a.m. he went to his official office in the Palacio de Gobierno.

Along with Leila, the brilliant woman who was Minister of Foreign Affairs, I was able to convince the President that we were not as lucid as he was in the morning, but that we each were fortunate to have Vice Presidents who were quite alert, and that the President should feel free to call them. My policy was pretty unusual because it's considered very important to be called by the President, especially if he calls you to his residence. But I needed to preserve my mornings.

I had two good reasons for not talking to the President in the morning. First, our situation in the Finance Ministry was so complicated and so ambitious, I really needed to focus. And my Vice Presidents knew the details that the President needed to know anyway.

Second, it was a good strategic process. If there was a critical public issue, like a strike, I would send the appropriate Vice President to consult with the President. Then the President and my staff member could buy time, think twice, slow things down, and not be railroaded into something. If I appeared too frequently at the side of the President in public, we would be bombarded with requests and pushed for an immediate response by the press or the interested parties. We needed time to consult before being questioned.

I learned that politicians had different interests than economic Ministers. Politicians were not so worried about producing good economic figures. But my mother had taught me very early on that you can only spend what you have. Our President was natured more like my father. If there are social needs, we promise to help. Later we'll figure out where to get the money to do what we've promised. These differences often led me to have serious debates with the President. He would tell me as we met in the government palace, "Ernesto, this is not a business.

Ernst meets Pope Benedict XVI. (Between the Pope and Ernst are the First Lady and President Duarte.)

We are not here to earn money by starving the population as you capitalists love to do."

The important thing was that we really understood each other. Whenever the President had to receive delegations of people who actually didn't need anything more than a kick in the behind in order to make them get to work, we knew we had to help them somehow. Our duty was to keep the famous "social peace." Otherwise, they'd strike. Our challenge was to lose as little as possible with them. But in those moments, my power of self-control was in serious danger. The President knew that. So we had an agreement that for those kinds of sessions, my very wise Vice Minister Gómez would replace me because he never got hot. He knew how to transmit the message that there was just no money available to help, that he'd love to help them but the Ministry was struggling with serious limitations, yet he'd give his best effort to convince the Minister that something must be done.

Of course, the President was always eager to make it clear that he was in charge. He would promise such groups some help, nurturing their hope that it could be even more, as long as there might be a possibility in the budget. That meant we had to reprogram the budget, cutting some parts while increasing others, and then getting the approval of Parliament for those changes.

So when we were faced with a complicated problem, I would call the President and tell him I was sending a Vice President to him. I would promise to come over later so that we could drink tea and think through the issue together. This approach was a bit unusual for Paraguayan culture, but I think it better served the Paraguayan people. My Vice Presidents were the experts on many of the details. They also served well as filters since everyone wants to speak directly to the most important person. They could explain to the people bringing proposals what further homework they had to do.

I had the fortune of having able and loyal people who worked 12–14 hours a day. I trusted them. If they had problems, I stood by them, and, when I needed them, they stood by me. At times, we literally cried together. Miguel Gómez was Vice Minister of Finance. Andreas Neufeld was Vice Minister of Tax Collection. Jorge von Horoch was Vice Minister of the Economy and Economic Integration. Max Rejalaga was Director of Public Purchasing. This teamwork within the Ministry of Finance, along with the support of the President and of many members of Parliament (who had to approve the efforts), made it possible to have four consecutive years of fiscal surplus during our administration—the first time since the beginning of Paraguay's democracy. It simply meant that the state was collecting more money than it was spending. For four consecutive years we also were able to achieve economic growth, also a first. In 2007, the growth was 6.8% higher than in 2006. (See "What We Set Out to Do" pages 192–196.) And the prospects for growth are very good for the next years. On August 15, 2008, the newly elected government will receive a country with financial matters in order and a surplus in the national treasury.

Certain principles helped me set the tone by which the Finance Ministry operated. I showed my lead staff the door through which people came into my office. I said, "Everyone who steps through my door and your door has a monkey—a problem—on his back. Their aim is that when they leave, their monkey will sit on *your* back. If you allow that, you'll break down by the end of the day with all those monkeys on your back. Our challenge is, What can we do to help each person take his monkey with him?"

We had brilliant specialized teams who briefed us before all important meetings. They helped us to know how people could take their problems with them and do their own homework. They helped to sort out which monkeys were ours to solve and which belonged to the persons who brought them. We succeeded in lowering a lot of unrealistic expectations. And we were able to deal with about 80 percent of the issues on the spot.

I work best when there's not a lot of high drama going on. So as a public person who was always being observed, I had to figure out how to handle the constant stream of problems and questions coming across my desk, while always being aware of how I was being perceived. The message I wanted to give was, We will solve the Ministry's problems within the Ministry and not on a public stage whenever someone uses drama to pressure us.

The tenser I am the calmer I appear. It's partly my nature. That frustrated some people because they thought I didn't care about their issues. I had a long and almost grievous learning process, for me a slow and difficult growing period, based on failed experiences.

Staying focused on the objective and the strategy helped me to calm down during tough sessions. And over time, I figured out that heated meetings weren't really that important. I found I could speak directly and with strength without offending the other party, as long as my tone and body language weren't insulting. I think I frequently frustrated some of the press because people entered my office angry and demanding but usually came out calm and satisfied.

At the beginning of our administration, our numbers were in poor shape in the eyes of the International Monetary Fund (IMF), and there were considerable tensions between the IMF and Paraguay. When things seemed calmer under my leadership, some of the press began to imply that the IMF had loosened its requirements on Bergen, when in fact, we had very tough negotiations. (See the IMF report on pages 190–191.) But I didn't scream insults about what was happening. Maybe one asset I have among my many deficiencies is to lead negotiations in tense situations and have a calm outcome. Many times my adversary would get upset with my apparent calmness. Yet my intentions were to work for win-win. But you can't do that based on baloney. I had a very good team who provided good background and facts to build on.

Of course, there was my encounter with Ña Eustaquia. She is a leader of one of the Red Party chapters, and she's headquartered close to the Parliament building on the river coast. There are rumors that she will provide "special services," even to Parliamentarians; in other words, that she knows the sub-world of her area well. In fact, she seems to know everyone important on the political scene. Over 60 years old, she is quite impulsive, is said to weigh more than 200 pounds, and has dyed red hair. At parties, she always manages to dance with all the party bosses. It is said that she carries her pistol in her purse, also while visiting with party leaders.

She had my private phone number, but I hadn't returned her calls. She told my secretary she *had* to talk to me. I knew that when she called, it was usually to ask for something that was not good for the whole country. But she is powerful in the Red Party, and she expects to be listened to. So she left some threatening messages for me.

One afternoon I got a call from the President on my private cell phone. "I have a big friend of yours here in my office," he said. Of course he knew I had tried to avoid her! "I'll put her on." Ña Eustaquia started yelling at me, saying that I "ignored important people." She went on, "The President receives me and you won't? I'm coming to see you now and if you don't receive me, I'll start a strip-tease in front of the Ministry. I'll take off all my clothes if need be." I started using my best political rhetoric. I said, "I'm waiting for you right now. Please come right away!" The President was dying laughing. Out of her hearing he said to me, "I know you're agreeing to meet with her now just because you're afraid of Lucy!"

When Ña Eustaquia arrived, I had to embrace her convincingly. I told my private secretary, Fernando, to "write down everything that this very important woman wants so we can give it very pointed consideration." Her list of wishes was pretty long. Eventually we were able to meet some of her demands, including a gift from my private business for a freezer. She actually needed that in order to store milk that the First Lady's Foundation had provided for one of her projects, which organizes the distribution of milk to needy people.

I had learned another lesson. Sometimes in government you have to do some small symbolic things—even theatrical ones—to ensure goodwill and cooperation. I didn't doubt for a minute that Ña Eustaquia would have followed through on her threat. She's very clever, and she'd have loved to appear in the papers, stripping in front of the governmental office of a very pious Mennonite Minister. Half an hour after Ña Eustaquia left my office, the First Lady's Foundation called Lucy to say that her husband had just suffered a terrible sexual assault! I must pay tribute to my assistant Fernando, who behaved as a perfect gentleman, making Ña Eustaquia feel very comfortable!

Chapter 13

Seizing a Moment

Last Good Friday, during *Semana Santa* (Holy Week), the President was in his *quinta* (his weekend house), and he invited me to come for a half day to discuss some matters. It happened that I arrived while he was with another cabinet Minister, who is also a close friend, and with a Parliament member from his party. Their topic? How to come up with a candidate from their party for the next election. The President was trying to convince the Parliament member to go along with his vision. I knew the Parliament member. He was very powerful, although some said he wasn't the most transparent. But sometimes he really tried to be.

At the end of the meeting about party business the Parliament member said, "I'd like to take advantage of the presence of the Finance Minister and the President himself and complain persistently and bitterly about the direction that the customs department is going. I've wanted to discuss this many times with both of you. It's affecting me personally, as well as many of our friends."

The President went right along with him. "We are listening to you. Tell us what's happening!" Nicanor was being very dramatic and showy. The Parliament member explained in great frustration, "In earlier times, the cost of getting containers out of customs was seven to eight million Guaraníes. Now, shame, it costs me between 18 and 19 million Guaraníes. We are almost approaching the same amount as if we were doing it legally! How shall we cover our political expenses?" In other words, the cost of a bribe was approaching the legal cost.

I held on to my chair because I was tempted to pick it up and hit him with it. It would have given me lots of pleasure! I thought of denouncing him publicly, but given his connections, I knew I'd likely not win a lawsuit. The President saw that I was trying to exercise self-control, so he said to the Parliament member, "I'm not sure I understand.... Why don't you explain this more fully?" And the guy did. The President said to me, "Mr. Minister, what's your opinion?"

I thought of playing it innocently. I thought, I'll say that I'm an outsider, a Mennonite, and I don't understand. By taking that stance I could probably say stronger things in response to him because he figured I was naïve and uninformed. In fact, he did elaborate further on his situation. Finally I said, "I think this is excellent, Mr.

President." Nicanor looked surprised and a little provoked at me. "How is this, Mr. Minister?" he asked. I said, "Mr. President, this great leader of your party is congratulating your government. Look what you've achieved—the government is now costing as much as bribes!" I went on, "What we hear here is great support of your work. We are on our way if the black market costs almost as much as operating legally!"

The President said, "So what do you recommend?"

I said, "Well, he's so close to being legal, why doesn't he just go legal? He'll sleep better." Growing bolder, I looked at the Parliamentarian squarely. "And, by the way, when you cooperate with the government, you are helping the poor."

The President turned to the member of Parliament and said, "I embrace you. You can be a model of entering the legal system." The Parliament member caught on that we were playing with him. He was eager to change the subject. He told me he was opening a new factory—which would work within the legal system, he clarified. He knew that my passion was production.

I was making progress in exercising my "contingency power," my self-control. If I managed not to become too stressed by responsibilities, I could find humor and creative solutions for all kinds of situations. The President so loved my explanation that the black market had caught up to the legal, that before the member of Parliament left he said to me, "Why don't you repeat that one more time so I'm sure I understand it?" He was trying to nail it home, and to send a clear signal to me and the Parliament member that he would support me and my principles.

I have to work hard in a situation like that to keep hold of my self-control and concentration, but at such a moment the President likes to joke around and play his black humor. So we were a good team.

Lucy was visiting with Gloria while this was going on. Later when we gathered as two couples, Nicanor told the women, "You won't believe what we just did." He recounted the whole story and made it even bigger!

There were small victories along the way, but the enormity of Paraguay's financial situation was never far from my mind. Along with my team, I became much more loyal to the rest of the cabinet, and together we forged a

The First Lady speaking in Belgium,
with Lucy (seated) to her left.

stronger commitment to work together for the betterment of the country. I often was able to operate with a sense of support from the government in the effort to do what was right for the people. Many times the President and cabinet were willing to pay the price, take risks, and give up personal benefits in order to strengthen our economy and bring about better conditions for the poor.

Through it all, I held firmly to two goals: to increase the overall national budget, and to increase the amount of social investment. The latter involved offering greater health services (the hospitals are owned by the government, and doctors are government employees) and health insurance, social security, educational opportunities (all public schools through grade nine are government owned), police and emergency services, welfare benefits, housing, as well as making land available to the poor at accessible prices. (See "What We Set Out to Do" in Part II, page 197.)

Because of Paraguay's fragile economy, and its history of a growing fiscal deficit and ballooning foreign debt, the International Monetary Fund watched any major financial move we tried to make.

In 2006 we had the honor of a visit from Anoop Zink, the Vice President of the Southern Conference of the IMF. The President of our Central Bank functioned as the nexus between the IMF and Paraguay. I was chief of our country's negotiation team. Nicanor was not very enthused about the IMF. Seventy percent of our population opposed the political solutions the IMF wanted to impose. But we couldn't ignore or discount the IMF. We needed their good reference to give us a good image outside of Paraguay and because they gave good support to our internal fiscal efforts.

The President was ready to receive the IMF group at 5:00 p.m. at his residence. He was in a pensive, reflective mood. We all showed up and were received and made all the introductions and talked about the big honor it was to be visited by this important man. I was trying to make the mood as positive as possible. But by then the President was saying, “I don’t understand why this International Monetary Fund is helpful for us. It’s like stamping a visa into our passport, but without giving us the money to travel. What good is giving our people visas, but no resources to travel?”

Apparently the Vice President of the IMF was accustomed to criticism because before I could answer he said, “I understand the frustrations you have. The Fund is going through an important process of being reformed. I’m sure that I can express some of your frustration and criticism into that process.” We all sat there open-mouthed and shocked because the President had begun the visit in such a blunt manner. His image of the visa without money was quite pointed, and he made no effort to soften it. We went on with the meetings and were able to sign some helpful agreements.

It was always important to the IMF that Paraguay had a balanced budget and no deficit. This was always my goal also. We understood clearly and believed firmly that an unbalanced budget with a deficit can do a lot of damage to the economy of a country. But it is not easy to achieve a balanced budget. I asked my Vice Minister Horoch, who was the liaison between the Finance Ministry and the IMF, and was leading the negotiations with my coaching, "Why don't those good IMF people who live so close to the White House just cross the street and ask the U. S. government how to have a balanced budget? And once it works for our friends in Washington, have them pass the recipe on to us!"

Horoch, with his great diplomatic ability, said, "Mr. Finance Minister asked me to speak on his behalf because he knows I received a good education in the U.S. He has pushed me to ask this question: Why doesn't the U.S. always follow its own rules? Could you help me explain this to him since he doesn't have much education?" Of course they didn't answer him, but evidently they got the message. I have to admit that the IMF did good work in our country, and they eventually gave us good ratings for the financial improvements we were able to bring about in Paraguay. (See the positive report by the World Bank in Part II, pages 186–189, and the supportive press release by the IMF in Part II, pages 190–191.)

Chapter 14

Power—And What to Do About It

I wasn't quite prepared for the amount of power I suddenly had when I stepped into government. Lucy thinks it's my nature to be fearless about a lot of things, but the power I had in government scared me. To be the Minister of Finance of a country, leader of the economic team, responsible in a certain way for the whole national fiscal budget, gives you mixed feelings—fear, responsibility, and power.

All around me I saw powerful people who had failed to handle power well. Typically, I look around to find someone I can identify with when I'm in a new situation. And so I looked for someone who was in government now, or formerly, who could be a model for me. I couldn't find anyone.

When I was in business, I came to believe that the more power a person has, the more responsibility s/he has to serve others. That conviction followed me into government, where it's been a strong burden of mine. Two questions have played continually through my mind. Where does power come from? How do I use it correctly?

I also wondered, Who gives power? Who takes away power? The President, supposedly, but is he really that powerful?

I believe that I am responsible to the people who gave me power. I also believe that power is delegated by God, or, put another way, that God allows people to exercise power. But I must admit that those two realities haven't always seemed to line up for me. So I studied the Bible and some other books on this issue. I reached this conclusion: God had given me power in order to serve him, to serve people, and to serve the institutions I was placed within.

This grid helped me to evaluate myself and others as we exercised power. It also clarified the relationships I developed with my colleagues and the level of affinity we had with each other. What I have experienced is that "responsibly held" power is never an end itself, nor is it given to persons simply because of their positions. Power should be directed toward the goals it's useful for. For example, I've come to firmly believe that God-given power is ultimately to help the needy. It must always be oriented toward service.

Prosperity is about as frightening to me as power is. A saying I've heard has bothered me a lot: "Out of a hundred people who can face adversities, only one can face prosperity." The phrase is troubling to me because I come from a very humble home. The President grew up very poor, too, as did many of the other cabinet members. How could we possibly be prepared to experience prosperity? I watched carefully to see how these people who were close to me managed their prosperity and their power. I saw people changing drastically once they had access to one or both. I witnessed amazing transformations around me. I saw how easy it is to commit serious mistakes, and I was eager to avoid them.

It's very normal for leaders to be overloaded. In stressful moments in the office, I often thought of another quote I had read: "A thousand cuts on the leaves of a tree of evil are equivalent to one cut at the root of the tree of evil." And usually on the heels of that, this one credited to Martin Luther would come to my mind: "I have lots to do today, so I need to spend another hour on my knees." I was not very good at spending hours on my knees, or much time in prayer. But I constantly asked myself, Am I spending time on the leaves, the visible expressions of evil, or on the root? It was important for me to stop the ball, the play, and see where I was at that moment. In practice, I went out to the countryside several times a week to walk an hour or two, and to drink *tereré*, in an effort to check out where I was standing.

As a child I couldn't understand why Jesus didn't heal everyone, and especially why he would leave sick people behind and take a boat across the lake. But as I held public office, I understood how essential it was to leave the noise and obligations so that I could retreat, pray, seek guidance, and try to get a clear picture of what was happening. I tried to stick to this discipline, and I think it prevented me from committing fatal mistakes which could have done me in. Often during a crisis, I'd take a half day to drive out and walk in nature so I could think more clearly.

Still, I'm very results-oriented. When I was depressed and wondering if anything I was attempting was worthwhile at all, I tried to remember that God asks for obedience in the first place, and not for results. To be able to plant and to be able to harvest—both are in the hands of God's grace. My duty was to do my job well, and that was to plant. Results would depend on God's grace. That attitude usually helped me in moments of crisis. But sometimes it was a real stretch.

Chapter 15

Itaipú – An International Sore Point

The Finance Ministry daily faced an abundance of problems which required resolution, and new challenges arose constantly and quickly. I did not need more work. In fact, there was one financial issue that I really didn't even want to think about because I knew it could eat up a huge amount of time and energy and probably produce no positive outcome.

Paraguay shares two bi-national hydroelectric power stations with its neighbors: Itaipú with Brazil, and Yacyretá with Argentina. These hydroelectric power stations provide Paraguay with all the electrical energy it needs. They are one of Paraguay's most important resources.

It also is no secret that the Paraguayan population in general believes that the arrangements Paraguay has with Brazil and Argentina are highly unjust. Paraguay's benefits from the power stations are small compared to Brazil's and Argentina's. A further injustice is that those neighboring countries buy *our* energy very cheap, far below market prices. Neither of the two treaties is favorable to our country. It is acknowledged by all three countries that both hydroelectric plants have quite a dark history. In fact, former Argentinean President Menem referred to Yacyretá as a "monument to corruption." That's why I asked the President to free me from everything related to Itaipú and Yacyretá. But it seemed that was not possible.

Technically, Paraguay owns Itaipú (linked with Iguazú Falls) 50-50 with Brazil, and Yacyretá (farther down the Paraná River) 50-50 with Argentina. The power plants were built with loans from Brazil and Argentina—and they each determined their respective interest rates.

Furthermore, the original treaties provided that Paraguay must sell any energy which it doesn't use to its partners in the projects. For example, Itaipú has 20 engines; Paraguay owns 10 of them, but needs only one to supply energy to the whole country. Paraguay is obligated to sell the excess energy to Brazil—at prices which Brazil establishes.

And so, according to the treaty, Paraguay sells its leftover energy to the Brazilian national distributor at a very low price. But that distributor sells it on to its Brazilian customers at market price. Paraguay, you see, is prohibited from selling to Brazil at market price.

Obviously, we needed to take a position which would do justice to the Paraguayan population. On the other hand, I was worried that if we did what seemed like the right thing and inverted the massive, easy income from these hydroelectric power stations, we may not actually promote the progress of our country, strengthen its economic health, or benefit the neediest sectors of our society. I had observed those nations with huge oil resources, especially in the Middle East, and seldom had their vast income benefited their citizens who were poor.

One of our most severe problems was the high interest rate that especially Itaipú paid to service its debt. The interest rate was more then double the average amount the Paraguayan state paid on its foreign debt. Once in a moment of utter frustration I suggested to the President that Paraguay should get an independent loan to pay off its debt to the Brazilian state treasury and that we should insist on selling our energy for realistic prices for the benefit of our people. In bilateral diplomatic relationships with Brazil we always included the topic of Itaipú on the agenda when the two presidents met. But it never came to any concrete resolution and the atmosphere surrounding the subject deteriorated.

Certainly, a complicating factor in the situation was the presence of "double indexation," a kind of surcharge which was added to Paraguay's already inflated interest. I knew that if I mounted an effort to bring about an equitable solution, I was facing not only the Brazilian government, but also the corporate culture of Itaipú. These "engineers" from within Paraguay, also known as the "barons of Itaipú," realized huge financial benefits in the way the loan payments were structured. So that's why I couldn't arouse much enthusiasm from select powerful circles inside Paraguay—both private and public—when I tried to push this agenda.

No question, there was considerable goodwill between Paraguay and Brazil at the highest levels. In our bilateral reunions and summits with Brazil's President Lula I felt that we shared a vision for a united Latin America. We saw a Latin America of brothers and sisters who cooperated and showed each other respect, where we acted on our consciences, and where the bigger countries saw the necessity of the smaller countries' well-being. During negotiations these attitudes prevailed in the heads and hearts of the presidents. It seemed that we should have a starting point for finding a resolution to this difficult matter.

A summit of the MERCOSUR nations' presidents was held on July 20, 2006 in Córdoba, Argentina. (MERCOSUR is the Common Market of South America.) One of the central topics in the bilateral reunion between Brazil and Paraguay was Itaipú and the so-called "double indexation." This troubling formula was arrived at by calculating a double interest rate: one rate at a "normal" level, plus a second rate tied to the inflation rate of the U.S. dollar. In my opinion, when these two rates were added together, the interest was shamefully high.

Since the presidents were looking for ways to advance toward a solution of this problem, President Lula asked to involve each country's Minister of Finance. In the Córdoba summit, Paraguay had expressed its disagreement with the double indexation being applied to the debt of Itaipú. So both presidents instructed their Finance Ministers to head up negotiations centered on finding a just outcome to the Paraguayan claims.

President Lula wanted to involve the Finance Ministers of both countries because the Brazilian national treasury is the biggest creditor of the Itaipú debt. My job, along with Brazil's Minister of Finance, was to find a solution to this "factor of adjustment" which was added to Paraguay's repayment of the Itaipú loan.

Because of the importance of the topic, we set a follow-up meeting to convene seven days after the Córdoba summit. We would meet on July 27, at the headquarters in Itaipú, close to the city and the wonderful falls of Foz do Iguazú. As we met in Córdoba, I thought I couldn't bear another headache like the negotiations around Itaipú. I was definitely convinced that I had enough challenges in the day-to-day management of the Ministry of Finance. I knew that we were facing an extraordinarily complex situation if we would try to achieve a change in the double indexation. There had been several previous—and unsuccessful—initiatives to solve the problem.

It was no secret that a lot of important people benefited considerably from the status quo. Some analysts believed that Paraguay could save more than 10 billion U.S. dollars in interest if we would be successful in readjusting the loan terms. The amount being charged to Paraguay was more than double the sum of Paraguay's entire foreign debt. The one thing we were certain of was that we did not want to pay this unjust debt. So who would pay it? It would not be easy to convince our Brazilian partner that it should assume that duty.

It was perfectly clear to me that I was heading into a problem whose dimensions no one could fully comprehend. And I never imagined we would go through such dramatic negotiations. I was walking on a minefield. Every mine belonged to a particular interest group, and they were not only Brazilian groups. Itaipú always had been a mine of gold for certain privileged Paraguayan individuals. So, as probably never before, I remembered and applied what I had learned in Sunday School in Psalm 50:15: "Call upon me in the day of trouble. . ."

After several intense and fatiguing meetings, first on July 27, 2006 in Itaipú and concluding on January 19, 2007 in Rio de Janeiro, we reached astonishing results. I sincerely consider the outcome to be a miracle or something like direct divine intervention. The Brazilian government committed itself unilaterally to eliminating the double interest rate, the so-called "adjustment factor," as the document on the following page, signed by both Presidents, shows.

Our Brazilian partners honored all their commitments, producing a law approved by the Brazilian Parliament (Law No. 11408/07), which backed up what President Lula had promised and signed.

I am sincerely grateful to President Nicanor for his constant support and loyalty during these negotiations. And I am equally thankful to the whole Paraguayan team who worked with me and proved their loyalty to our country during these complicated negotiations. But I must also express my gratitude to President Lula, whom I consider a man highly capable of integrating statistics

MEMORANDUM DE ENTENDIMIENTO ENTRE
EL GOBIERNO DE LA REPÚBLICA DEL PARAGUAY Y
EL GOBIERNO DE LA REPÚBLICA FEDERATIVA DEL BRASIL
SOBRE ASPECTOS TÉCNICOS Y FINANCIEROS
RELACIONADOS A LA ITAIPÚ BINACIONAL

Las autoridades de las Cancillerías y de las áreas económica y de energía del Paraguay y del Brasil se reunieron a lo largo de 2006 y en enero de 2007, con miras a buscar soluciones para un conjunto de temas relacionados con aspectos técnicos y financieros de la Itaipú Binacional.

Se trataron, entre otros temas, de los encargos financieros representados por las cláusulas de ajuste de los saldos deudores (factor de ajuste) de los contratos de financiamiento firmados entre Itaipú y ELETROBRÁS, y de la contratación de los servicios de electricidad de Itaipú Binacional en los términos del Tratado y de sus Anexos y actos complementarios.

Las discusiones permitieron alcanzar el siguiente entendimiento:

El Gobierno brasileño asume el compromiso de tomar todas las medidas necesarias, en carácter de urgencia, para suprimir el factor de ajuste en los contratos de financiamiento Nros. ECF-1627/97, ECF-1628/97, ECF-1480/97, celebrados entre Itaipú y ELETROBRÁS.

Río de Janeiro, 19 de enero de 2007

NICANOR DUARTE FRUTOS **LUIZ INÁCIO LULA DA SILVA**

and economic realities. The same is true for my colleague Guido Manteiga, the Brazilian Minister of Finance and his team, and for Celso Amorin, the Brazilian Chancellor and his team.

I learned some important lessons from living through this experience. Even though Paraguay is a small country in the process of development, we should not automatically yield to, nor become hostile toward, our partners and neighboring countries just because they are a lot more powerful than we are. The good guys are not always on one side and the bad guys on the other side. Respectful and firm negotiations can correct many injustices. And on the way to seeking a just resolution, one can often find a bigger portion of goodwill than expected. Of course, successful negotiations have their rewards: perseverance; increasing one's self-control, patriotism, and integrity; and developing a readiness to overcome problems and impasses. No one can guarantee that there will be a good outcome. But even that is not so bad, because recognizing that possibility fosters humility.

Chapter 16

Seeing the Big Picture and the Little Picture at the Same Time

---

In 2007 we knew we were entering a tough electoral year. It was the fourth year in the President's five-year term. People knew in general that the macro-economic situation had improved considerably. But we didn't want to nurture false expectations of prosperity. So we had not used fanfare in the press to announce our record tax collection success, or the excellent fiscal results in the economy. We recognized that, by making such a decision, we were giving up an opportunity to generate a good image for our work and for our Administration.

The President, however, was not fully convinced of this strategy, and he and I were having a severe debate. I asked him to stop referring publicly to our macro-economic achievements, because I thought that would lead to a lot of problems in our effort to reduce spending. He told me, "Ernesto, this is my government. I have won the elections. These results have been possible thanks to my support. And now you ask me not to announce them. Ernesto, don't forget that the center of power of the government is here [we were in the Palace] and not in the Ministry of Finance."

I replied, "Mr. President, you have emphasized that the most important thing in a soccer game is the final score. If you want to conclude your government well, we need to make this sacrifice now in order to finish the game well." The President understood and accepted my point. He did not mention macro-economic results in his public speeches for as long as I was in office (which turned out to be the next six months and 29 days). This was crucial support for the Finance Ministry's work.

Of course, the data is public, and employees in my Ministry could see it, so most of the public employees thought this was an opportunity to ask for a salary raise.

One day while I was giving a press conference in the Palace someone asked me, "Mr. Minister, will there be a salary raise for the public employees?" It was a topic I had certainly not planned to cover at that time. I told the audience that I understood the economic needs of the employees, but our resources didn't allow for a general salary raise during that year. The next day's headlines read, "Bergen Says No to Salary Raise for Public Employees."

Since the press had now brought the topic into public conversation, I asked the President to call for an urgent meeting with the cabinet. We reached a convincing conclusion about why no salary raise was in store for 2007. We covenanted this together, reinforced by the President, that no department of the government would ask for a salary raise for its staff. But that did little to stop a wave that had been set in motion. The employees of my department were those who most understood budgets and they argued, "If just *our* department got a raise, that wouldn't change things much nationally. We could re-program the budget and make it all work." A strong labor union operated within the Finance Ministry, and they picked up this argument to a great degree.

We met considerable objection from segments of the public employees, especially in my ministry. They continued to pressure me and presented me with this picture: "We are the best organized department; we have produced the best results; and when the President talks, it's always about what we in the Finance Ministry have achieved. In fact, you always say yourself that our ministry's good results are thanks to us, and we have been able to save money in various parts of the department."

The ministry's staff did think that they were the best, that they could increase their salaries without impacting the budget, and that they deserved raises. I knew they were right. They were entitled to earn more than many other public employees, considering the work they had done. But when I held firm against the pressure, they took all their proposals to the press. The next day's headline? "Employees of Finance Ask Bergen for a Raise." Now I had to explain that their arguments were correct. They were due a raise. But they needed to understand that if they got a raise, the rest of the more than 200,000 public employees would think they deserved a raise, too. I said clearly, "It is not possible to give raises, and I hope the Finance Ministry employees understand that we need to consider the well-being of the whole population." The next day's headline? "Bergen Says 'No' to Salary Raise in Finance Department."

The Ministry staff threatened to strike. So we entered tough legal negotiations, with the press always eager to inform. Our negotiations were not successful. The labor union resolved to strike while Paraguay was hosting both the summit of MERCOSUR nations' presidents and finance ministers, as well as the full MERCOSUR meeting. The members of MERCOSUR, in addition to Paraguay, include Uruguay, Argentina, and Brazil, and associate members Chile, Venezuela, Bolivia, and others. The union called the strike to be held during the summit. Paraguay was pro temp of MERCOSUR. Doubling the public embarrassment and pressure was the fact that the Ministry of Finance was to be highly involved in the event since this Common Market is a financial union.

I anticipated this action and this timing because my guys were good, and they knew about strategy! They planned the strike to happen during the summit, which happened to coincide with the end of the month when paychecks normally go out. Of course, the strikers were not working, so certain employees and retirees didn't get paid, which only heightened the tension.

My Vice Minister, Andreas Neufeld, and his team had been very successful at collecting taxes. By doing this, they had more than doubled the fiscal income in less than four years. Remarkably, Andreas had stayed in that position longer than anyone ever had since the beginning of our democracy. But on Wednesday afternoon, June 26, one day prior to the strike and summit, Andreas Neufeld was served a subpoena by the state prosecutor to appear in court for an absurd reason. Things immediately got very complicated.

Even though I could legally keep Andreas in his Vice-Minister position, he had lots of detractors who wanted him out of office because he was so good at his job and touched the interests of important people. So I called Andreas in and suggested that he step down.

Within my first circle of advisors, we understood that we would have to think about a successor in time, considering the risky work we did. Andreas agreed completely with me about all of this. But this dramatic meeting was almost overwhelming, so full of profound pain and a terrible sensation that evil prevails over good. Prior to this, Andreas had assured me on several occasions, "I am prepared for the worst. I am willing to go to prison for this cause if it helps to formalize and legalize our economy."

During a difficult time when threats were being made, he had once called me and said, "Señor Ministro, I thought the worst thing might be to go to prison. But now I realize that it is worse if I get killed. I'm prepared for that, but it doesn't feel very good when I think of my family."

Andreas had exceptional support from his wife, Rita, and his family. Now I had to tell him with deep sorrow in my heart, and even with the possibility that I might be wrong, "Considering all that's happening, the bravest thing for you to do at this moment might be to step aside." Andreas understood the circumstances and that this was the time to resign.

That evening, I, together with the Minister of Foreign Affairs, Rubén Ramirez, had to host a banquet for all the MERCOSUR Ministers of Economic and Foreign Affairs who were attending the summit of member countries. Earlier in the day I had called the President to tell him about the situation with Andreas and to say that I thought a personnel change was needed. Only the President could make such a change. He was in a very important meeting and couldn't see or talk to me at the time. So he called me an hour later—*while* I was hosting the banquet!

I asked my visitors' pardon and tried to explain to the President the strategy I had worked out with Andreas. This was the first time I had proposed changing Vice Ministers. He approved my plan, but he wasn't with me wholeheartedly because he appreciated Andreas very much.

I went back to attend to the visitors. Half an hour later the President called me again. He asked me to come to see him because he didn't feel good about the decision. I told him, "I'm at an important meeting; may I come later?" He said, "Please come now because this is a crucial topic for me." The meal was about to be served at the banquet.

The Paraguayan Foreign Affairs Minister welcomed the MERCOSUR dignitaries formally. I sat for one minute. I knew I had to find a way to tell my colleagues that I had to leave the banquet which I had invited them to attend. I said, "The President has asked me to meet with him because of a small national inconvenience. In fact, if you want to see me tomorrow, you'd better set me free to go now!" I apologized very much and left. Of course, they understood this kind of situation from their own experiences.

The President was still eating dinner when I got to his residence. He said good-bye to Gloria, and we sat down together in his living room.

The President said to me, "Ernst, I don't agree that Andreas should step out of office. I am not at peace with that action. I will speak to his defense publicly tomorrow. His subpoena does not seem right to me at all."

I tried to show him that it might be a good time for Andreas to leave, that the planned strike would cause polemics, and that we had prepared a good successor. We had a kind of tense exchange of words.

The President said, "I want you to take full responsibility for what you are about to do. Andreas has been absolutely loyal, and I'm not in favor of this."

He asked me, "How will Andreas take it?" I replied, "I talked with him and he understands." He said, "Does he agree or not?" I said, "He understands."

He said, "I hope you know what you're doing." I said, "Why don't we call Andreas in?" We agreed that we would let the decision up to Andreas.

Andreas arrived and sat down. It was close to midnight. He showed the President the subpoena documents, and the President became quite convinced that the charge was totally trumped up. He started a long lecture about why Andreas should stay. The President got excited and emotional. I dared to interrupt him several times. He told me, "Please shut up, Ernst, it's my turn." He promised he'd publicly defend Andreas.

Finally, it was my turn. I told Andreas to look at the whole situation. I said it might be the time to step down. Finally, I prevailed and the other two agreed. There was a strong consensus in the end, despite the President's concern. We resolved that at 6:00 the next morning, we would meet with Gloria Páez, Andreas' replacement, with whom he had already talked. We called a news conference for 6:30 a.m. to announce the change; the press begins work at 4:00 a.m.

Perhaps the most poignant moment, as we faced the press, was Andreas publicly reassuring his nine-year-old daughter of his innocence. Old enough to grasp some of the accusations against her father, she had asked him if they were true. I realized again clearly that our children are not immune from the dangers experienced by those of us in public life.

I finished the dramatic news conference and prepared to start the MERCOSUR summit with the visiting Presidents and Ministers.

But first I called my office. They told me that the Finance Ministry employees' strike was on. The union had announced that no employee would be permitted to enter the Ministry building. I had instructed my first circle of staff to be in their offices at 4:00 that morning. Fortunately, they had been able to enter the building at that hour.

The strikers had been given alcoholic beverages in disposable cups (so no one would know that it was whiskey). They also had been given raw, rotten eggs to throw at our colleagues when they would try to enter the building. As the newly named Vice Minister hurried from the press conference to her office of tax collection, she was pelted with a rain of eggs as she entered the building. She is very good at evading attacks, but she couldn't avoid all of the eggs thrown at her head. Of course, everyone wanted

Ernst (far end of table on left), seated next to the President, addresses the Ministers of Finance of the MERCOSUR and associated countries.

to witness how the new person in authority would cope with this experience. Gloria Páez simply said, "Eggs do a lot of good to hair. So, now that I've had mine washed, let's get on with our work."

The strikers had also rented a powerful sound system, thanks to "gifts" from some willing "friends" who wanted to cause havoc in my department. The speeches began early in the morning and continued all day—and they were not the most favorable to me!

I was sitting next to our President at the summit. My staff briefed me every 15 minutes on my cell phone about the strike. I was looking very attentive, but my mind was elsewhere. As the MERCOSUR meetings went on, I tried to coach my team who were in a very tough battle. I repeated that we were promising no increase in salaries.

The tempo of the strike was rising. The police got involved. Some strikers were taken to the hospital. The actions were violent and tough.

Day Two. Public servants may strike, but they must ask for permission to strike, and they are required to request an exact length of time for their strike. The ministry staff had asked for only two days. The strikers knew this was their last day and that they'd have to reach a resolution because the foreign summit was ending and the weekend was coming. They were still loyal in their hearts to the Finance Ministry, but they wanted to try for better wages. Yet they realized that time was beginning to play in my favor.

During the second morning, one of the employees in our Information Department was able to enter the building. By megaphone the strike leaders asked her to come out, or they said they'd come in and get her. They were threatening to take the building by violence, to destroy the interior, and to take out the employee. I was with the President preparing details for the second day of the MERCOSUR summit.

The President is very experienced in managing a strike. He called the chief of national security and gave orders to send in as many water tanks as necessary to prepare to disperse the people. He asked the chief to command the operation personally. "You wet them all; you flood them with tear gas if necessary," he told the commander of the national police, Fidel Isasa.

At noon, the strikers informed me that they would extend the strike if I wouldn't negotiate. I said, "Please go ahead. You know I won't change my mind. Once the summit is over I will personally take charge of fighting your effort." They understood my strong message.

That afternoon the union invited us to a meeting. They voiced a list of conditions. We let them know that as Finance Minister I wasn't willing to sit down with them if they insisted on conditions in advance. We resolved together to form a commission to study a salary raise.

They finally agreed to lift the strike. We had assured them that there would be no recriminations or retaliation against them. I went to the office to talk to the employees. The old-age pensioners were worried that they wouldn't get their checks if the strike continued, so that helped turn public opinion against the strikers. But neither did the strikers want to damage the pensioners. Tense and intense give-and-take between the labor union and the negotiators on behalf of the Finance Ministry helped us advance.

Friday afternoon, two hours after the declaration was signed and the strike was lifted, I went to my office to receive the leaders of the two labor unions within my Ministry. They stepped in, looking tense. I tried to greet them in a very relaxed manner, although my mind was remembering the phrases they had used to describe me the day before. I need to say, however, that they had always shown me considerable respect before and during the strike, far better than my predecessors had received.

I opened by saying that they were right, doing my best to break the ice. Thanks to their work, the Finance Ministry has had good results, I said. I reminded them that I had made the same statement at the press conference. And I assured them that I understood their requests and agreed that many of them deserved a salary raise. But I pointed out that, at this moment, we all had to prioritize the needs of the whole country over their private needs, and so we would have to postpone a raise. I asked for their understanding. Then I told them that I wanted to place a challenge before them. "You are people with long careers in this Ministry, and I thank you for all your support. But I ask you, could you name any Minister who has been able to achieve more labor benefits for you than I have since the beginning of Paraguay's democracy in 1989?"

I was meeting with a group of 17, six from each of the two unions and five of my closest co-workers. I shared my determination with them to fight for as many benefits as I could. "If you know of a Minister who has achieved more, I will go learn from him," I told them. They agreed that what I said was true and asked me to understand their situation. And they said, "This is just the best political moment to get benefits for our people." They added an emotional element, telling me that they had co-workers who were nearly going hungry, who couldn't send their kids to school, who simply didn't have enough money to live adequately.

They underlined that the President always pointed to the achievements of the Finance Ministry and that they were willing to work harder and achieve more. If I was willing, they said, "We can fix this." They also offered, "We know you're a personal friend of the President and that he will appreciate the goodwill of the opposition. If you use your good relationship, we'll use our good connections with the opposition in Parliament."

I was aware that these union representatives had negotiated with some friends of the President to get a direct audience with the President. I also knew that the President was willing to receive the group because he wanted to cooperate with the situation. But the President knew my perspective. I had told him, "Don't even think of receiving them at this time, as some politicians have urged. Instead, I will coordinate a meeting of my employees with you. This will be more helpful than involving some opportunistic politicians as intermediaries, who sometimes look for benefits for themselves in a crisis."

The union officials knew I had stopped their meeting with the President. But now they were insisting on getting a promise directly from the President if I wasn't willing to meet their demands. So I offered them this deal—"I will coordinate a meeting with the President for you, but meanwhile, you must establish peace and goodwill among your members. If a mood of threats and pressure persists, there will be no meeting with the President."

Things calmed down temporarily. Seven days later, the union officials and I met together with the President. I could always play the outsider when the President dealt with his party leaders. After lots of insider-party greetings and talking—when the group was warmed up—the President said, "This is such an important matter, let's put the salary increase off until next year's budget when we can deal with it in a fuller way." So in that meeting we reached a consensus. There would be no salary raise in this fiscal year, but we could give several additional benefits and still stay within the budget. Together we would work hard to get a salary raise in next year's budget and have it approved by Parliament.

The President was a wonderful help in solving the problem. He spent considerable time talking about party achievements and mutual friends, all the while telling me about how effective these people were! After an hour and a half of small talk, he convinced them that he understood their needs, and he made a commitment to get the raise into the next budget. To the credit of the union leaders, I must say that they displayed a great willingness to help solve this delicate situation. And the President and I also wanted to find a win-win outcome for both sides.

I learned a lot from managing this crisis.

I felt a more profound respect and love for the employees of the Finance Ministry. I believed that the vast majority wanted the best for all.

I saw the importance of creating an environment of loyalty and trust with one's employees and maintaining that especially in times of crisis.

In times of crisis one gets to know better one's own character and that of others', too.

Labor union chiefs need to achieve results in order to hold their power. And they need to manipulate people sometimes to do so. That's expected; otherwise, their reason for being fades.

In complicated negotiation processes, it's important to go beyond the status and the role an institution prescribes for you until you reach a more human relationship. In this situation I tried to go beyond my position as Finance Minister and become Ernesto. And the union leader became Pedro.

I believe that these are essential ingredients if you want to generate a winning position for yourself and the other party, especially when the press is waiting outside the door for word of a tense showdown. I tried to stay focused on the ultimate objective and rely on my always-helpful team. A sense of timing, and not losing control of the timing, allows you to be generous as you negotiate.

I didn't set aside my position as Minister or act offhand about it. At the same time, I didn't flaunt my power. I believed that in the crisis, both sides would lose if we seemed to be having a bloody confrontation. We would also lose our good reputation as a Ministry. In short, all of us would lose if we couldn't find our way through this. A fight, a split, a bloody story would not help either side. When the union leaders began to sense that, and when I had convinced them that I wanted them to win, too, I could become a human being to them. Then we could talk about timing and about how and when to approach the President.

The experience was an important lesson in crisis management for me. Through it I also developed a clearer strategy about forming public servants. I have come to believe that their *commitment* to the well-being of the nation is most important—it is Number One—and their capability stands right beside their commitment.

Chapter 17

Deciding to Leave – Without Knowing the Future

One of my objectives when I entered government was to not get stuck there. I had asked God to keep me from becoming intoxicated with power so that I'd be able to distance myself from the office at the right time.

I had become chief of the government's executive team. I had been in office longer than almost any of the other current cabinet ministers, or previous ones, and the Ministry of Finance was one of the most powerful. In the preceding 14 years I was the Finance Minister with the longest tenure.

In May 2007, I had an exceptionally brilliant staff in the Finance Ministry. And, after a severe crisis in the Central Bank, we had established a very good team there.

(The Bank plays a similar function as the Federal Reserve Bank does in the U. S. Structurally, the Bank communicates through the Finance Ministry to the President. The Bank is independent, yet it needs to work through the Ministry.) Economic indicators in that month were the best in the 18 years of Paraguay's democracy.

We were well on our way in preparing the national budget for 2008 (one of my main jobs), and the economic results of 2007 were becoming clear. We were anticipating that the new budget would set forth clear objectives, prior to receiving the refinements and interests of the other Ministries. I knew a big battle was coming about salary raises in many departments. We would not be able to increase wages in 2008 because that would create a fiscal deficit, inflation would rise, and if some salaries were raised, others would agitate for increases in their pay, which we simply couldn't afford.

While many things were looking up, I also realized that I, along with my staff, had been moving very fast, and a vehicle that is constantly on the move, especially while bearing a heavy load, wears out. I was aware that a very powerful wave of opposition to my vision and personality was on the horizon. The political atmosphere was being affected by the coming election, and both were feeding into opposition against me. I had made many unpopular decisions. Anyone determined to win against the current government had to attack prominent persons in that government. I was in line for that. It was a good time for highlighting our achievements, but particular interest groups would also attack our policies. We had touched many sensitive areas in our efforts to do away with tax evasion.

However, my major preoccupation was not the criticism I might get, nor the difficult moments I might face. What I was worried about was the quality of my leadership when I knew I was extremely worn out. Would I be able to give what the country needed?

I had become deeply tired, accumulating a lot of fatigue. I had started needing some medication to sleep and to do my work. I came to a moment when I wasn't sure if I had enough power of self-control to restrain myself. Recognizing the powerful position I had, I wondered if I might be capable of causing major damage or a catastrophe in the event that I wasn't able to keep myself under control.

God reminded me of two things. Great leaders in the Bible and throughout history committed terrible mistakes when they were over-stressed and lost self-control (like Moses). Also, I had preached in my business that the cemetery is loaded with people who considered themselves to be irreplaceable and indispensable. So I started telling myself, There are others who can do the job better than I can. And I believed that.

Once this truth clicked in my mind, I started focusing on how I would make sure that the well-being of the Paraguayan people would be secured when I left. Most opinion polls presented me as the second best-accepted Minister, topped only by the Education Minister, who later became a candidate for President. I had convinced the public and private businesses that the economy would not be harmed during the election process. The papers themselves said this; it was a widely accepted opinion.

One day I recalled a statement that earlier impressed me—"You know a good leader by the way the institution continues to function after s/he has left." I observed, too, that the real work of the church began after Jesus left and his followers began to do what he taught.

During those days in May I started taking longer walks, and I began to write a first draft of my resignation letter. It was the first that I had attempted doing this because it was my conviction never to use resignation to threaten others. I wanted to see how my body would react. I felt much peace in this process, so I continued. It was clear to me that the one who would succeed me should be better than I. Good teachers know that their students have to do better than they have, and will also go farther. If this weren't the case, how would there be development in humanity?

So for the next 60 days, during June and July, 2007, I entered a process of preparing my leave.

I had three main concerns. I did not want the economy of the country and the well-being of the people to be harmed. On the contrary. I wanted improvement. I did not want to dishonor the President with my leaving. He had always been extremely loyal and supportive of my work. And I did not want any false interpretation that the government would now have a looser grip on the finances because of the upcoming election.

I began working on two fronts. First, I prepared my resignation letter, especially considering how I would approach the President with the news. That would be difficult. I also tried to figure out the best way to communicate with the press so that the people would understand. Second, although it's obvious that the President decides who to name and who to dismiss, I knew I would need to suggest some candidates who would be capable of holding the line on a number of actions and be able to get better results than I had. The President would want the new Minister to continue what we had been doing. And since s/he would be finishing my term, s/he would have only a bit more than a year in office.

Once I had put some of the pieces together, I started to talk with Lucy. I began talking with very close friends, confidentially, testing with them what I had in mind. They all supported me.

I invited the board of elders of my church to meet with me, as I had when I first considered becoming Minister of Industry and Commerce. I wanted to have an *asado* (a grill party) at our weekend house on Thursday evening, July 12. Lucy prepared a great meal. And the elders helped me analyze four aspects of my decision in the form of questions: 1.) Is my involvement in the government an authentic expression of service and Christian testimony, and will it continue to be in the next months? 2.) Will my resignation damage my friendship and supportive relationship with the President and his wife? 3.) Will my resignation endanger my future? Will it damage or hurt my businesses? 4.) How heavy is my current stress on my marriage and my children?

The answer to the first question — Yes. The answer to the second question — Maybe, but I would do everything possible to prevent this from happening. The answer to the third question — There is a considerable amount of risk involved, on both the personal and business levels. The answer to the fourth question — Yes, my wife and children are bearing too much of my stress. In fact, they have had to make considerable sacrifices because of my stress.

Ernst with his daughter, Daniela, and his older son, Samuel.

The counsel and guidance of my local congregation has always been very important to me. I wanted their wisdom when I considered entering government and when I was leaning toward leaving government responsibility. The reason that I didn't go to them first as I contemplated resigning was because I wanted to have cleared away the technical issues before talking with the elders. The church was fundamental to my decision, and I didn't want my mind clogged with smaller concerns when I consulted with our congregational leaders.

The meeting with my pastors was very helpful, and, as a result of those conversations, I was able to correct some of the procedures I had planned. In the next few days I followed up by phone with several of them to clarify my next steps.

On Friday, July 20, I asked the President for a relaxed and quiet meeting. We agreed to meet Sunday afternoon. I arrived at his residence with my "schoolbag," as he calls it. We sat down. And then the show started! He said, "Have you come to collect something from me?"

I said, "I've come to analyze what we've done so far and how the future might look. I've prepared a report—let's look at it together."

I had prepared an extensive list of what we had achieved so that he could see what a good position the economic sector was in. He didn't suspect anything. When we got to the bottom of page one he interrupted me. "What are you here to preach at me about? Do you think I'm not pious enough?" He was smart enough to sense that something else was coming, so he had "opened the umbrella" to be prepared for whatever it was. I went on to page two about the future, emphasizing the good people and the strong teamwork we were enjoying in the economic area. He sat looking at the page, beginning to see what was coming. Then he said, "Finish what you have to say, and then close your folder. Everything will stay the same. Let's talk about another topic."

But I went on to page three where I addressed my personal situation. I had been in power for 47 months—26 in Finance, and 21 in Industry and Commerce. When I came to the place in my paper where I thanked him for the opportunity to serve, and he saw my signed resignation, he stopped me and said, "Have I failed you? Please tell me so I can correct whatever it is so we can stay together through the end of my term."

I assured him that he had done nothing wrong to me. He replied, "You can't do this now. How will you communicate this to the press? Everyone will think there are ulterior motives, that something else is going on."

I said, "In the folder is a strategy for how to address the press and deal with public opinion." I had written my proposed speech and showed it to him. (See Ernst's letter of resignation, translated into English, on pages 199–203.)

The President and I are friends. We have a high level of trust, so he thought he must have done something to cause my decision. The meeting with the President on that July Sunday ended with him asking me to take my folders with me. I insisted that I felt I should resign and that he should be the first to know and to hear it from me. I said good-bye and asked him to reread my report and to continue to talk with me about my request and the future of the Ministry.

The meeting was one of the most difficult ever for me. It burdened my heart because I was seeing a good friend struggle. I had a bad night. But I was convinced I was doing the right thing.

The next morning I went early to the office. On my way, the President called and asked me to see him in his office in the Palace. I went directly. We had a very understanding and cordial conversation as friends. I promised the President that I would support him and work for him from the outside as much as I could. And I would do everything possible so the team at Finance would stay.

After talking for a long time, we were ready to evaluate possible candidates. We soon agreed on one of them. The President asked me to call him as soon as possible and ask for a meeting. A very big stone fell from my heart. If I could have, I would have jumped to the top of the government Palace!

The candidate we agreed on was César Barreto. He was currently President of the Finance Agency of Development, a new institute we had created to finance development in Paraguay. We had appointed him two years earlier, and he had achieved amazing results. I called him and said, "The President wants to talk to you." He asked, "What's the topic?" I replied, "I guess it's best the President tells you himself." He said, "I'm on my way." It was to be a meeting alone between César and the President.

When the meeting ended, he called me and told me, "Mr. Minister, you got me into trouble." I replied, "I don't think so. I believe our President has a great vision for the future."

César and I had worked together well. We set a meeting and started talking. I handed him all the critical information he needed. He was processing the offer and hadn't agreed to serve. I encouraged him to accept the invitation and explained why I was about to leave. Like me, he was not a politician and did not belong to the government party. He wanted to know if there was tension between me and the President because of that or anything else.

He told me that on Thursday, July 26, the Agency of Development would celebrate its one-year anniversary, highlighting the agency's brilliant achievements. He promised to give an answer on Friday, the day after the event. Finally, on Saturday morning after some back and forth, he accepted the position of Finance Minister. We agreed to help each other and to convince the whole team at Finance to continue with him.

I then met separately or in groups with all the leading staff people—20 of them. From Friday evening through late into Saturday night I explained why I was leaving and why I wanted them to stay. I was thankful that they understood and were willing to trust the new person. On Sunday morning we called the whole leadership team of the Finance Ministry together, along with the new president of the Finance Agency of Development, Hilton Jardini, who was replacing Barreto. The meeting was to start at 9:00 a.m. At 11:00 a.m. we would make the public announcement about my resignation and the appointment of my successor.

At 9:00 we had a very emotional meeting with the President leading us. I thanked everyone, especially the President, and I clarified that this was a very private decision. I had no controversy with the President; we would remain friends. The President spoke and said that nothing would change in the economy. Together we thanked

Barreto for being willing to step in. Barreto thanked the team for staying and the President for his loyalty. Many of the others spoke words of gratitude and commitment. And then we left for the news conference, headed by the President.

This was a major event with considerable impact because it was the first time in Paraguay's democracy that the Finance Minister had changed without any rumors or pressures. It was the first that there was a great sense of continuity, where the whole team stayed and worked with the next Minister.

For me, it has been a good ending. The new Minister has been well received by the Finance Ministry employees, the public, the President, and the other ministers in the government. In our private conversations the President says, "Things are going very well."

I am also grateful that the public, as well as the people I worked closely with, accepted the change without blaming the President or me, or without undermining the leadership of the President. That possibility had concerned me. We wanted to prevent my leaving from being interpreted as lack of loyalty or trust in the President. Some speculated that my departure would damage public trust in the President's leadership. Others credited me with holding the government together because the President was perceived to be very political. But no disasters happened.

Ernst on the beach with his son, Samuel.

Entering government is like a plane taking off on a flight. But every pilot realizes that landing is another critical moment of high risk. I had that in mind from the beginning of my time in government. I had to have a plan for landing.

Have I learned anything from these four years in public life? That nature has its way and that's good. It's our job to sow, plant, and cultivate, but God gives growth and fruit. I felt very privileged to see God's grace in action, to have been part of something that turned out well. I'm perfectly aware that this isn't guaranteed. I know people who have been sowing and cultivating better than I have, but haven't had the privilege of seeing the results of their work.

I think a lot about my parents, who continue to be very important to me. They are extremely happy people, although they have no earthly power and very little money. But they're a model of contentment—thankful for their family and health, sacrificing their lives for other people. They're enjoying this stage of life with their friends. I want to end my life with the deep peace I see in them.

I'm very conscious of how many leaders fail. I'm working constantly at defining the meaning of success for myself. I've come to believe that the most important thing one can accomplish is to be able to say that I've done what God asked me to do. Jesus said he had done that—glorified his father—and I think that's the most I can do.

I'm still not good at studying, although I read a lot more than I used to. My body seems fragile; I take medication whenever I travel. I'm very conscious that to succeed I need others. I depend on the gifts, resources, and professionalism of other people.

I speak a lot about these things with Lucy. Together we are trying to teach our children to have tender consciences, to experience a sense of community. Lucy and I are praying for them and praying with them. I want to be a good model, including admitting my mistakes in front of them. I should improve much more as a father. During my time in government I didn't give our children enough time and attention.

Lucy has done an exceptional job of being a parent and has tried to cover for my shortcomings. Thank God, I have a good relationship with our children, Daniela (18), Samuel (15), and David (5). I talk with our daughter about her boyfriends—diplomatically, I think. The important thing is that we strive continually to seek for the best way.

My congregation, especially my brother and his family, remain very helpful. Until 2005, my brother Holly was pastor of our congregation. Since then, he pastors a sister congregation. We are neighbors and live very close in many ways. Our congregation has been very supportive and has had quite a mature relationship with us along the way.

During this in-between time since leaving the government and before stepping into something new, I've come to see myself more clearly. I know one of my weaknesses is that sometimes I make decisions too quickly. I'm trying to improve in that, and Lucy helps me a lot with this. I've been learning, especially while in government, to listen to many sides of an issue, to hear things I haven't thought of and considered.

Another thing. Usually when I make a decision, I stick to it. And sometimes people have gotten hurt by my determination and stubbornness. I'd like to have more patience. I don't listen sufficiently to people. I get a picture of what's happening, and then just go forward with it.

I'm very hard and demanding with my co-workers. Some people can't live with that and they leave. Those who stay tend to be very loyal. I'm also very demanding with myself. I'm not sufficiently careful with human relations. I can be very obsessed with getting the right result. I don't greet people enough and ask how they are doing. Schmoozing doesn't come naturally for me. And I'm a bad public speaker, although I'm in the process of learning. But it still exacts a big price from me.

I've always been impatient. I used to think it might have been because I was driven by money. But I'm the same way when I'm in a situation that has nothing to do with money.

In many cases, idealism is a problem for me. I don't know which I am—not idealistic enough, or too idealistic. Maybe I'm a frustrated idealist. My work in government rubbed hard against my idealism. Many times I couldn't accomplish what I wanted to. I've discovered how hard it is for an idealist to receive critical comments.

The President says that criticism is like blood and a doctor. A person who can't stand blood can't function as a doctor. If a doctor sees blood, he wants to heal. In the same way, someone in politics has to see criticism as a sign of something needing healing.

I'm less of an idealist now than I was earlier. I think it's a little like raising children. Now I don't know anything, when before we had kids, I had all the answers.

In spite of all my weaknesses, I am at peace. One of my ongoing prayers is that God will continue to give me peace. I'd like to grow in this. God has helped me not to grow ambitious with money—and I was very ambitious. I've come to understand that from a certain level up, money has nothing to do with happiness. I've learned that one wrong decision can lead to losing a lot of money, while another decision can lead to making lots of money. And I've learned to know how fine the line can be between those two choices.

What's next? Until the end of President Duarte's term, I promised to be available to help the President and the Finance team from the outside as much as I could.

Upon the recommendation of my mentors, I have not returned to executive management and leadership in my businesses. The businesses are doing very well, and I could become more of a problem than a solution if I started getting involved in them again. The presidents of the businesses took a great commitment on their shoulders when I entered government. It would simply not be right for me to reclaim the presidencies, trying to change things and putting these current leaders aside.

I do try to give some counsel and contribute toward strategic planning. But mainly I focus on social projects and the social responsibilities of entrepreneurship, areas that fascinate and enthuse me. Lucy sometimes complains that I don't work less since resigning from the government. I think she exaggerates a bit.

I left government because I was burned out. When I resigned, I was one of the last Ministers originally appointed by the President who was still with his administration. As I've said, I was the longest-serving Minister of Finance in any of the last three governments. If I were ever to return to government, it wouldn't indicate that I've had a fundamental change in my understanding and convictions. But I also know that the only certain thing in politics is change...

Ernst and Lucy in Europe.

Epilogue

From Intensive Care to Intermediate Therapy?

The early months of 2008 were stormy politically. I stepped out of the Finance Ministry just before the election campaign moved into a crucial stage.

From then on, whenever Nicanor called me to come and see him, I felt light as a feather. In the same rooms and easy chairs where we had had heavy meetings and had to resolve complex issues, I was filled with relief. I could take the role of a friend. When he asked for my perspective or advice, I was willing to be available.

The Colorado Party went through a bloody internal election campaign, trying to determine its official party candidate for the general election. With a tiny margin of 0.5%, Blanca Ovelar, the Minister of Education, was selected as the Colorado candidate. The whole process left the party with severe internal wounds, making party unity for the general election almost impossible.

We knew that Blanca's chances of being elected were not the best. Although she is a woman who cares deeply for the Paraguayan people, has worked hard in the area of education, and comes from an honest and humble family, it was a major stretch for the Colorado Party to put forward a female presidential candidate for the Paraguayan nation. There was a considerable amount of resistance to her candidacy. And it took her a while to fit comfortably into the expected role of public and popular speaker at election campaign rallies.

April 20, 2008, the day of general elections, came closer. The polls we were receiving indicated that Blanca's chances were not very strong against her principal rival, the bishop Fernando Lugo. He was positioning himself as a candidate for a wide alliance of opposition parties and social groups. We believed that the perspectives held by Nicanor and his team, and the serious work we had begun in 2003 toward fighting poverty and inverting social structures, could be continued in a second period with Blanca as president. Of course, the future of the party was not my priority. My battle was to fight for the welfare of the country.

On Election Day a radiant sun came out. We were blessed with good weather and a people who voted with discipline, peacefulness, and a strong exercise of democracy. There was serious concern about outbursts of violence, but that disappeared when a swift counting of the votes gave a clear victory to Lugo. Blanca, the losing candidate, congratulated him, admitting her defeat just a few hours after the voting polls closed. The international observers and reporters were amazed at how well voting procedures were handled, with almost no incidents or accusations of deception. I attribute the peaceful and the undisputed results to the many prayers of believers. Nicanor also had the humility to congratulate the President-Elect on the evening of the election. I have no doubt that for months, and maybe years, Nicanor will be strongly accused by his party of having lost its political power.

Today, a few weeks later, I see similar challenges, but also differences, with the period beginning in April 2003, when Nicanor became President.

More then ever I am convinced of the maturity, kindness, and dignity of our Paraguayan people. We leaders

Left to right: The First Lady, Lucy, Ernst, the President and his youngest son, together in Europe.

would be well advised not to try to manipulate them or to believe that they are ignorant. These last elections showed more than once that such mistakes are politically expensive. Our people are mature enough to sort out promises which are impossible to deliver.

Early on in his administration, Nicanor convinced the Paraguayan people, and the politicians, that if our country was to change for the better, everyone would need to help. The new government has this same opportunity. If they are wise enough to make national needs a priority, I am convinced that the people will enthusiastically join in the work we have to do. This is what I most hope for the authorities who will assume their responsibility on August 15, 2008.

Five years ago we told the public that our nation was in intensive care. That really was our situation then. We began working with seriously negative social and economic difficulties. Thanks to God (and for me this is not an empty phrase), we were able to achieve amazing macro-economic results. We were also able to make progress toward some social inversion and in creating a more responsive general economy. In the course of five years, we developed a steady, although tense social peace. And we began to bring a more formal structure to the economy and to the functioning of the national government.

Today I believe that the patient is in intermediate therapy. The country has had a very favorable evolution, considering the emergency state it had been in. But it would be a fatal error to think that Paraguay has fully recovered, that it can be dismissed from watchful care. Neither has it yet regained physical, emotional, and spiritual health so that it can function without major intervention and support. We have the opportunity for a very satisfactory recovery. We do face the danger of sliding backwards fatally, or recuperating only halfway, which could allow us to survive, but without securing the hoped-for quality of life that the nation and the people deserve.

Perhaps now more than ever we must practice what U.S. President Kennedy once said: "Do not ask what your country can do for you. Instead, ask what you can do for your country." Electoral victories and new governments create great expectations. Humans seem to have a deep wish to see miracles and to believe in miracles. And more than one politician has been tempted to promise miracles. But history shows us that real transformations, and those that survive, need the effort and participation of all.

I am inspired by the leadership style of Nehemiah, the Old Testament figure. His great gift was to motivate all the discouraged Israelites who lived in the ruins of the destroyed Jerusalem to start working again. After he described Jerusalem's dire situation to the whole nation, he reminded the people about the good hand of God which would be with them. Then he announced the program of reconstruction. The biblical text says, "They replied, 'Let us start rebuilding.' So they began this good work" (Nehemiah 2:18).

When we began five years ago, we sometimes felt like we were jumping into empty space. Looking back now I can see that the empty space was never bigger than the hand of God which held us.

Part II

BEHIND THE STORY

Caribbean Sea
Caracas
VENEZUELA
Atlantic Ocean
GUYANA
SURINAME
FRENCH GUIANA
Bogota
COLOMBIA
ECUADOR
BRAZIL
PERU
Lima
La Paz
BOLIVIA
Sucre
Brasilia
Filadelfia
GRAN CHACO
PARAGUAY
Asuncion
Itaipú Dam
Yacyretá Dam
Pacific Ocean
ARGENTINA
Santiago
URUGUAY
Buenos Aires
Montevideo
CHILE
Atlantic Ocean
Falkland Islands
0 275 550 Miles
0 275 550 KM

A Brief History of Paraguay

by Alfred Neufeld

The nation of Paraguay has a fascinating, but also tragic, history. In 1539, Paraguay was "discovered" by Europeans, and the capital, Asunción, was founded. On the way to Peru, Spanish conquerors entering the Rio de la Plata wanted to find a shortcut to the legendary "El Dorado" and the gold of the Incas. But Pizarro had beaten them there, and so, greatly disappointed, they settled down in the Asunción area. Fortunately for them, a segment of the large Guaraní Tupí tribe, the Carios, lived in the area. They had beautiful daughters and were looking for a strong ally against their traditional enemies, the Payaguás from the Chaco and the area around the river.

And so, with the arrival of these Europeans began the most intense creation of Mestizos—or "mixed blood" peoples—in all of Latin America. A Catholic priest of that time complained in a letter to Spain that concerning polygamy, the Asunción area was worse then any Muslim country. Mohammed allowed up to seven wives, but any Spaniard who did not have up to 70 beautiful Indian girls as wives would be an exception, he wrote. Today, close to 90% of the Paraguayan population descends from the mixed blood of Spanish and Guaraní ancestors. Paraguay is the only country in Latin America in which the aboriginal language, Guaraní, has dominated the Spanish language, and where the Mestizos were stronger than the Spaniards from their very beginning.

What followed the arrival of the Spaniards is a history of deceptions. The Indians who gave their daughters felt betrayed, the center of power in the region moved to Buenos Aires, and Paraguay became a landlocked, back-country, impoverished province.

The Franciscans did their best to keep the Indians quiet and happy with their lot of poverty. The Jesuits were expelled after their magnificent effort to recover the dignity and well-being of the Indian population.

The first movement seeking independence from Spain started in Asunción in 1811. But it ended with the extraordinarily cruel dictatorship of Dr. Francia. Development and industry began to flourish in the 1850s, but that came to a dramatic end during the Great War of the Triple Alianza, which Paraguay and its neighbors Argentina, Brazil, and Uruguay fought from 1864–1870. Genocide resulted. At the end, there was only one male for every seven females, and Paraguay had lost half its territory.

The democracies which developed between 1900–1940 brought, for the most part, unbearable political instability. The military regimes which followed and lasted until 1989 were even more frustrating. Roa Bastos, the most prominent Paraguayan novelist, once stated, "Bad luck (*el infortunio*) seems to have fallen in love with Paraguay and is not willing to abandon us."

Historically Paraguay has had an agriculture-based economy, growing cotton, beef, sugar cane, and, lately, soybeans and sesame. There is a sizable population of about 300,000 impoverished small farming families, many of them having no land in recent years. They are selling their small properties to big cattle ranchers and large soybean planters and ending up in the slums and streets of cities.

Since World War II, two political parties, the Liberals (blue) and the Republicans (red), have each been struggling to become the predominant political power. The Red, or Colorado, Party has successfully held office for the last 60 years. Now the Liberals have attracted a wide spectrum of support from Socialists to high-society liberal-market advocates. The same is true for the Republicans, who have recently defined themselves as humanistic Socialists, and historically have been very close to the humble and populous masses. In any case, both groups have fanatic members.

Rafael Barrett, a Spanish anarchistic journalist, stated 100 years ago that since the two parties have very little real differences in their ideology and doctrine, they have to differentiate themselves by the colors of their flags and scarves. Even at that time he complained that the Paraguayan population was infected by a "political virus": "Those who do not live from politics and from public money feel a patriotic zeal rising in their blood, and they launch themselves into political struggles in order to capture the power."

Today Paraguay has a population of a little more than 6,000,000 people. The country has lived through 19 years of struggling, but improving, democracy, with a very free press, no political prisoners, and elections that are becoming more transparent, due to inner and outer pressures and control.

About the Mennonites of Paraguay

by Alfred Neufeld

Mennonites came to Paraguay as refugees. They came for several reasons. In the 1920s, a group of somewhat conservative German-Russian Mennonites wanted to leave Canada because the government was starting to restrict the independence of their traditional German schools and was questioning the non-militaristic position of their churches. Since Paraguay wanted to attract good farmers and was looking to install population in the central Chaco (whose ownership was disputed by Bolivia), the Paraguayan government granted the Mennonites a generous special law in 1921. This so-called "Mennonite law" guaranteed religious and school liberty, as well as freedom from military service. A group of these "cultural refugees" from Canada founded Menno Colony in 1927 on land owned by an Argentinean company, but inhabited by Enlhit Indians.

The second stream of refugees came for more political reasons as a result of the Bolshevik Revolution in Russia. A considerable number of German-Prussians in Russia miraculously managed to get out of the Soviet Union on November 25, 1929. Since this minority group wasn't welcome in Canada, Mennonite Central Committee, a North American relief and service organization, helped them find passage to Paraguay. Together with additional help from Germany, the refugees were able to form Fernheim Colony in the central Chaco in 1930.

During these years, Mennonites and related groups immigrated to different parts of the country, including the eastern part of Paraguay. Those who settled there soon started a vigorous missionary outreach, resulting in Mennonite churches among indigenous groups of Enlhit, Nivaclé, Guarayos, and Ayoreos, as well as the majority Latino Mestizo population all over Paraguay.

Today, Mennonites with immigrant backgrounds have become very strong socially and economically. The average per capita income within their communities is more than 10 times higher than the national average. At the same time, the Mennonite mosaic of churches has become quite multi-cultural. In fact, the whole community of Mennonite faith, including a multitude of ethnic groups, is finding new and dynamic ways to integrate and interrelate.

They share theological training and a university; a media presence with radio and television stations; economic and political engagement, as well as sponsorship of the Mennonite World Conference Assembly in Asunción in July 2009. Together, these activities give a somewhat significant profile to Mennonites in Paraguay. All of the Mennonites total about 1% of the Paraguayan population, making Paraguay one of the countries with the highest proportion of its people belonging to this church tradition.

Most would agree that the Mennonite settlement in the central Chaco has contributed decisively to the economic and social development of that area. Even the building of the Trans-Chaco road, so crucial for the Chaco's productivity and integration, was strongly motivated and supported by the Paraguayan Mennonite community, as well as the legendary "Pax boys," young North American Mennonite volunteers who helped build the road in the 1960s.

Since 1950 there has been an efficient ministry to leprosy patients throughout the Eastern part of Paraguay, headquartered in the Hospital Menonita Km 81. Participants in Mennonite Voluntary Service work with residents in the national old-folks home and with patients in the national psychiatric hospital, as well as providing homes and education for street children and single mothers in Asunción.

Immigrant Mennonites from Russia brought their economic cooperative system to Paraguay. The Cooperative Fernheim 1937 was the first one to be registered in the country. Today the agricultural cooperative system is one of Paraguay's strongest economic factors, having spread its strength through all segments of society.

Inspired by evangelism, and with the strong support of the North American Mennonite Central Committee, a large economic development program was established between the immigrant communities and the native ethnic groups of the central Chaco. Today this agency, called ASCIM (Association of Mennonite Indigenous Cooperation), has developed quite sustainable community organizations, methods for healthy social change, and strong agricultural production, as well as programs in public health and bilingual contextualized educational systems. A similar organization, MEDA (Mennonite Economic Development Associates), is providing supportive finances and small agricultural and industrial opportunities to marginalized populations. The "Mennonite business chaplaincy" of Asunción has been active in helping Mennonite entrepreneurs reflect about business ethics and in strengthening the social and the pastoral responsibilities of companies owned by Christians.

Since the overthrow of the Stroessner regime in 1989, the more active presence of the government and its democratic procedures has had a strong impact on the Mennonite immigrant communities, as well as the native ethnic groups surrounding them. For decades, both societies lived practically with an absence of the state and government. Both communities are now in a process of integrating more visibly into the national society, including actively participating in election campaigns and social security systems, running for public office, and affiliating with one of the national political parties. Nevertheless, it was quite a novelty in Paraguayan history when the public realized that First Lady Gloria Penayo de Duarte, was a committed member of a Mennonite church and that in 2003, the new President's cabinet included several Mennonite professionals and businessmen who had had no previous political careers.

As with social change anywhere any time, the new Mennonite activity presents opportunities as well as dangers.

World Bank Report

Paraguay Country Brief, September 2006

DEVELOPMENT PROGRESS

After almost a decade of economic stagnation and a recession that began in 1998, economic growth in Paraguay recovered during the past three years. The return to positive rates of growth, which averaged 3.5 percent between 2003 and 2005, has been supported by policies that have focused on restoring confidence in public institutions, stabilizing the fiscal accounts, reducing debt, and embarking on structural reforms in a number of areas including revenues, public sector pensions, and the financial sector. Global and regional conditions were positive during this period, including exceptionally high commodity prices that spurred expansion in the Paraguayan agricultural sector.

The renewed emphasis on fiscal stabilization and on the fight against corruption and informality has had a particularly positive result in the area of revenue collection. The customs and tax administrations increased tax collection by a cumulative 45 percent between 2003 and 2005 (well over 20 percent in real terms). This, and restrictions on wage and capital spending, have returned the fiscal accounts to surpluses since 2004. On the external front, Paraguay's exports have risen significantly, driven by the exports of commodities such as soy, and more recently, meat. This resulted in current account surpluses during the 2002–2004 period, but in 2005 an import boom led to a negative current account balance.

Unfortunately, social indicators have not enjoyed the same improvement as macroeconomics and fiscal numbers. The recession of 2001–2002 led to a large increase in poverty rates from 34 percent to 46 percent of the population, with extreme poverty rising from 14 percent to 24 percent of the population during the same period. Conditions have improved with the recovery in economic growth, and in 2005, poverty and extreme poverty are estimated to have declined to 38 percent and 22 percent of the population, respectively. Employment rates have risen, with a corresponding reduction in unemployment, although the bulk of this growth is concentrated in the informal or rural economy.

On the political front, the country is preparing for a series of elections beginning with those for municipalities in November of this year and closing with presidential elections in mid-2008.

CHALLENGES AHEAD

Paraguay's main challenge is to return to a path of significant and sustained economic growth, one that can translate into improved living conditions and access to services for the poor. Notwithstanding the recent upturn in growth in 2003–2005, average Gross Domestic Product (GDP) growth over the past decade (1995–2005) is only 1.5 percent per year, significantly below the 2.4 percent population expansion rate. Paraguay ranks as one of the poorest Latin American countries, with high income inequality, low access to post-primary education, and poor indicators of health and basic infrastructure services. In addition, there are large disparities in human development and access to services between rural and urban areas. Despite the recent boost to GDP growth, Paraguay is unlikely to achieve most of the Millennium Development Goals by the year 2015 without accelerating progress in economic and social conditions.

Although important achievements have been made in educational attainment and coverage, particularly initial and basic education where coverage was 90 percent in 2002, significant challenges remain. Enrollment in grades 10 to 12 was 32 percent in 2002, one of the lowest rates in Latin America. Completion rates are low, with dropouts concentrated in low-income rural areas, and the quality of education continues to be a problem. The coverage of health services is low, and there are difficulties in supplying health services, particularly in terms of ensuring their equitable geographical distribution. A significant proportion of Paraguay's citizens, around 10 percent, live too far from healthcare centers to benefit from them. The concerns over equity and coverage between rural and urban areas in both education and health pose the challenge of how to reduce the concentration of financial, physical and human resources in urban areas.

Conditions are similarly difficult in infrastructure, and needs in both the transport and the water and sanitation sectors are high. By regional standards, the state of large portions of Paraguay's road network is poor. Resources available for maintenance cover only about a quarter of the network's requirements, conservatively estimated. Coverage of water supply and sanitation service in Paraguay is low and lags behind other South American countries, although SENASA (the entity responsible for rural water under the Ministry of Health) has been making significant strides in increasing rural water supplies with funding from various donors including the Bank. The quality of wells, surface reservoirs, and latrines is poor in many parts of the country. In addition to the need to maintain existing infrastructure assets, coverage expansions and service quality improvements are urgently required if public infrastructure is not to become a bottleneck to Paraguay's growth and social development.

International Monetary Fund Press Release

Statement by an IMF Staff Mission to Paraguay

Press Release No. 07/178
August 8, 2007

Mr. Alejandro Santos, mission chief of the International Monetary Fund (IMF) to Paraguay, issued the following statement today in Asunción:

"A mission from the International Monetary Fund (IMF) visited Asunción during the last two weeks for discussions in the context of the fourth review under the Stand-By Arrangement (SBA), approved by the IMF Executive Board in May 2006. The mission met with Finance Minister César Barreto, Central Bank President German

Rojas, other members of the Cabinet of Ministers, and senior government officials.

"The economic expansion continues and real GDP growth is expected to accelerate from 4.3 percent in 2006 to 5 percent in 2007, supported by a strong agricultural recovery. Headline inflation has fallen as the supply shocks of late 2006 unwound, and core inflation continues to be below the 5 percent target for end-2007. The fiscal position remains strong with good revenue performance and continued strict control over expenditures. The balance of payments has been stronger than expected, and reserves rose to over US$2 billion at end-June 2007, while the exchange rate has stabilized.

"The authorities' program is broadly on track. All quantitative performance criteria for end-June 2007 under the IMF-supported program were observed with substantial margins. Implementation of the structural agenda is also generally on track with only one structural benchmark still to be completed (the design of a strategy to strengthen the financial position of the Central Bank). The staff will remain in contact with the authorities on this pending issue and expects to complete the discussions for this review shortly.

"The mission would like to thank the authorities and the citizens of Paraguay for their assistance and warm hospitality."

What We Set Out to Do

prepared by Paraguay's Ministry of Finance

We have set out a 3.5% GDP average annual growth since 2003 until 2008

The GDP growth was 6.8% in 2007.

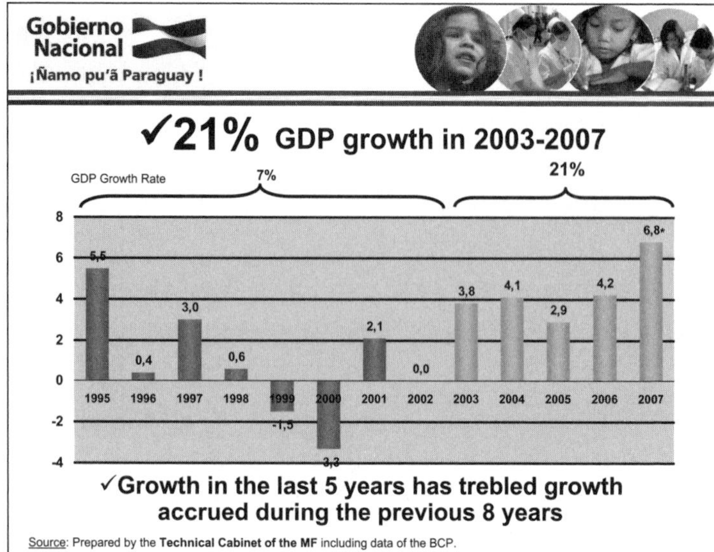

We have set out to increase exports by 23% since 2003 until 2007

193% exports growth have taken place since 2002 until 2007.

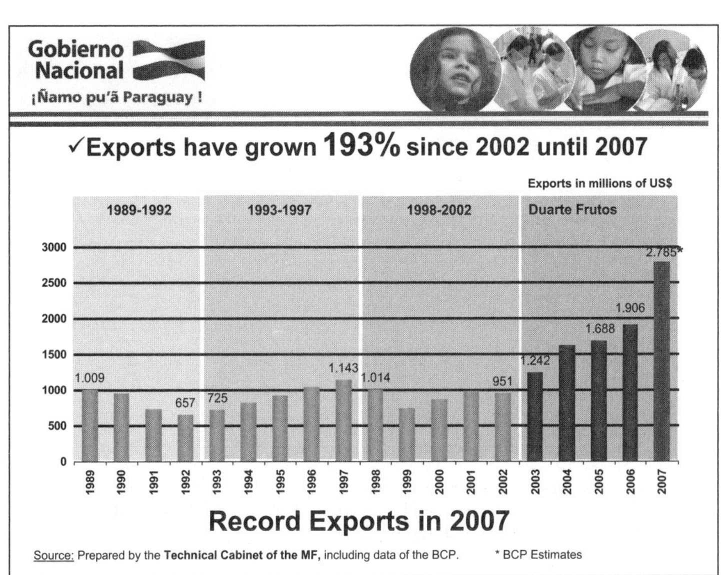

We have set out to reduce the External Debt to 35% of the GDP

The Public External Debt has been reduced to 18.6% of the GDP in 2007.

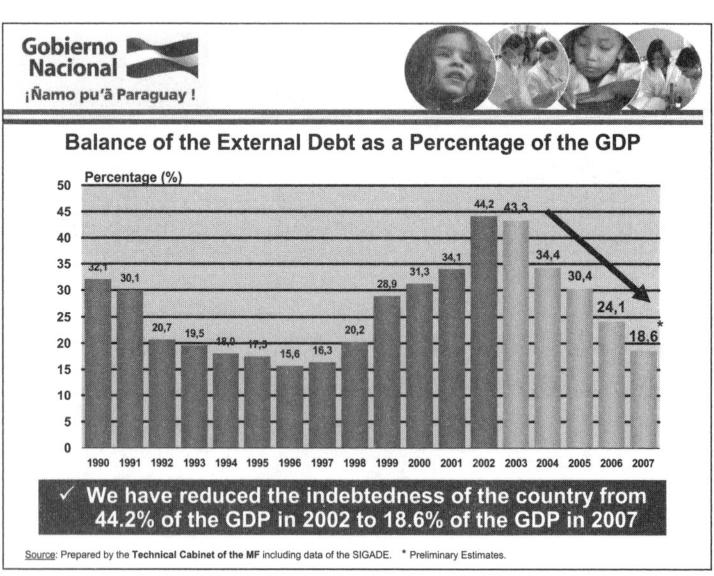

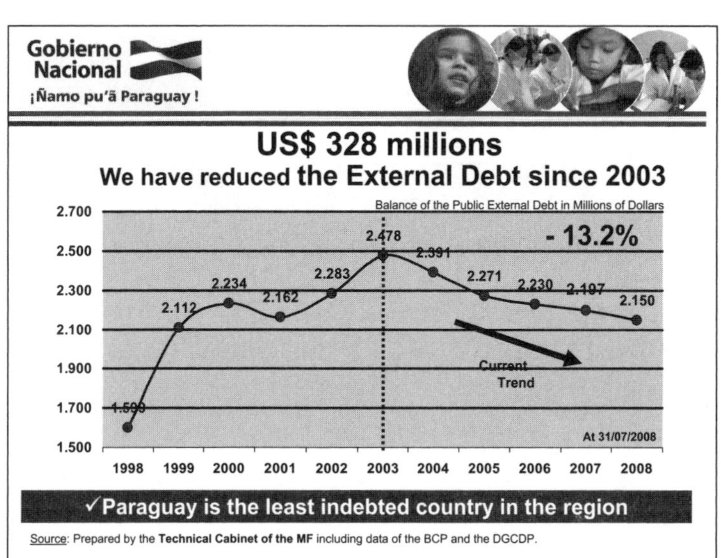
Gobierno
Nacional
¡Ñamo pu'ã Paraguay !
US$ 328 millions
We have reduced the External Debt since 2003
Balance of the Public External Debt in Millions of Dollars
- 13.2%
2.700
2.500
2.300
2.100
1.900
1.700
1.500
2.112
2.234
2.162
2.283
2.478
2.271
2.230
2.150
Current
Trend
At 31/07/2008
1998 1999 2000 2001 2002 2003 2004 2005 2006 2007 2008
✓Paraguay is the least indebted country in the region
Source: Prepared by the Technical Cabinet of the MF including data of the BCP and the DGCDP.

Gobierno
Nacional
¡Ñamo pu'ã Paraguay !
We have set out to increase Capital Assets imports.
Capital Assets have increased from 28% in 2002 to 46% in 2007 considering total imports.

We have set out to increase the international confidence in our country.

The rating of the long term sovereign debt of Paraguay improved from "Selective Default" to "B", according to Standard & Poor´s.

Rating Evolution of Paraguay

Debt Type	Background	Current Situation*
Long Term – in Dollars and Guaraníes	2002: C 2003: **SD (!)** **2004: B-**	**2007 rate** **B**
Short Term - in Dollars and Guaraníes	2002: B- 2003: **SD (!)** **2004: C**	**2007 rate** **B**

Source: *www2.standardandpoors.com*

*Rating Preliminary Report - June 2007

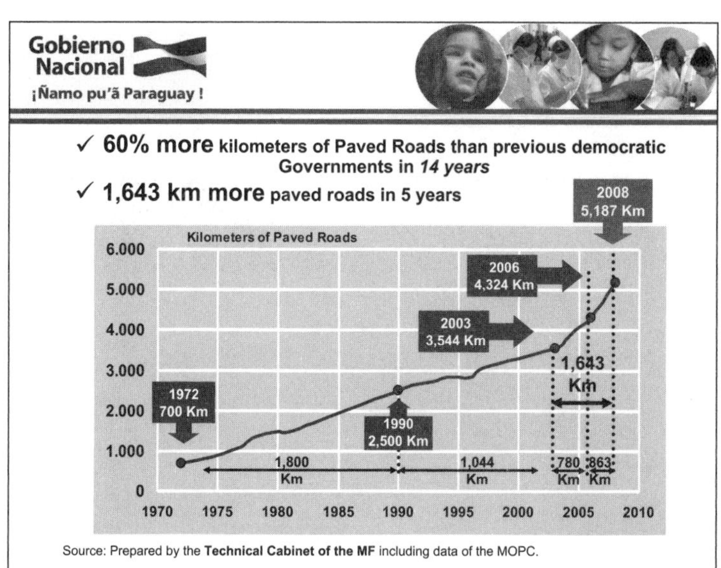
Gobierno Nacional
¡Ñamo pu'ã Paraguay !
✓ 60% more kilometers of Paved Roads than previous democratic Governments in 14 years
✓ 1,643 km more paved roads in 5 years
Kilometers of Paved Roads
2008 5,187 Km
2006 4,324 Km
2003 3,544 Km
1990 2,500 Km
1972 700 Km
1,643 Km
1,800 Km
1,044 Km
780 Km
863 Km
6.000
5.000
4.000
3.000
2.000
1.000
0
1970 1975 1980 1985 1990 1995 2000 2005 2010
Source: Prepared by the Technical Cabinet of the MF including data of the MOPC.

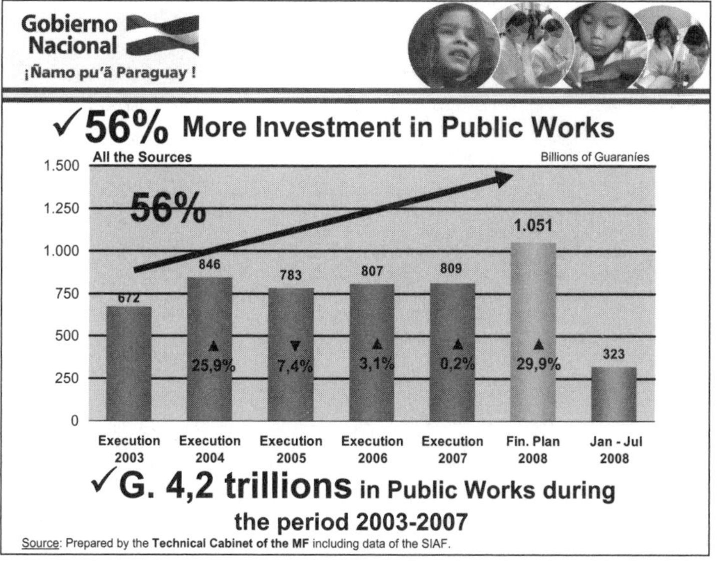
Gobierno Nacional
¡Ñamo pu'ã Paraguay !
✓56% More Investment in Public Works
All the Sources
Billions of Guaraníes
56%
672
846
783
807
809
1.051
323
25,9%
7,4%
3,1%
0,2%
29,9%
1.500
1.250
1.000
750
500
250
0
Execution 2003
Execution 2004
Execution 2005
Execution 2006
Execution 2007
Fin. Plan 2008
Jan - Jul 2008
✓G. 4,2 trillions in Public Works during the period 2003-2007
Source: Prepared by the Technical Cabinet of the MF including data of the SIAF.

Asunción, July 22, 2007

Most Excellent
Mr. President of the Republic
Don Nicanor Duarte Frutos

Mr. President:

I am thankful for the opportunity you have given me to cooperate with your government. I value the support and the trust that you have always given me.

This has allowed me to serve the people of Paraguay, giving back in this way some of the many good things I have received from God and from our great country.

Out of personal reasons today I present my resignation from the office of *Ministro de Hacienda* [Ministry of Finance].

I wish your Excellency wisdom and blessings from God to govern our country in the best way possible for our people.

With greetings of respect,
Ernst Ferdinand Bergen

Achievements in the economic area by the government of Nicanor Duarte Frutos—July 2007

1. The government of Nicanor Duarte Frutos has achieved astonishing results in the economic area: stability, a fiscal surplus, low inflation, record in social investment, record in federal reserves, a stable dollar, record in export and import with the perspective of a record of growth of the gross national product of the last 15 years, reduction of poverty etc.

2. Today this government has a positive fiscal result in the first half year of close to one billion Guarani, representing an improvement of more than 20% compared to the surplus in the same period in 2006.

3. There will be additional income of 45 million Guarani for this year from Yacyretá [the hydroelectric plant co-owned with Argentina] and $72 million Guarani from Taiwán between now and the end of 2008.

4. Today this government has one of the best teams of human resources and professionals staffing the *Ministerio de Hacienda*/Ministry of Finance. The same is the case in areas related to the *Ministerio de Hacienda*/Ministry of Finance: the Central Bank of Paraguay, the financial agency of development, the Banco Nacional de Fomento, as well as many in the customs offices. The results achieved witness to this affirmation.

5. I consider this to be so, thanks to God's blessings and thousands of prayers prayed by the Paraguayan people. I would like the honor and the glory to be given to God.

Future

Wisdom is the capacity to use the best means,
in the best moment, to achieve the best goals.
(According to *Santa Biblia de Estudio para Líderes*)

Mr. President, you have a clear political objective, and that is to win elections in 2008, in order to continue to achieve your vision for your country.

To win these elections and to continue with your vision for the country (the goal), there might be more suitable people (means) for the moment that we are living.

Personally, I consider you a great president, and history will recognize this with more clarity in the future. It has been a great privilege for me to work with you.

My personal situation

I'm sure that in the life of a man there are different time periods, and I consider that my time period as *Ministro de Hacienda*/Minister of Finance has come to an end.

After 26 months in office, and after being the *Ministro de Hacienda*/Minister of Finance who has held this office longer than anyone else in the last three governments (beginning in August 15, 1993), and while leaving a fairly positive economic situation in general, and while having a great team in the economic area as you have in your government, I believe this to be a suitable moment to step back.

I have to admit that I feel accumulated exhaustion after more then 47 months in government. This situation generates some limitations and increases the risk of making wrong decisions with a great impact, which would damage your government and our people.

I am thankful for the opportunity you have given me to serve our people. Your loyal support in any moment has been crucial to achieve important success. In a special way I value your friendship and your trust, and I appreciate the great opportunities to have learned a lot.

I am willing to cooperate in the transition period with the new *Ministro*/Minister, if that would be needed.

In the immediate future I feel that I should not go back to leading my businesses. I will search and clarify the future of my life by prayer and by listening to the counsel of my family and my friends.

Out of respect to you and your family, I will not cooperate in the elections of this year with any other political candidate.

My wish, together with Lucy, is to continue to be your co-workers, and in that sense my wife would like to put to the consideration of Gloria her office of Vice-President of the REPADEH [the First Lady's Foundation, *Red Paraguaya para el Desarrollo Humano*/Paraguayan Net for Human Development]. But she is also willing to continue to cooperate as she has done until now.

With Lucy, we value our deep friendship with you and Gloria, and we hope to continue to be your friends. We wish you wisdom and blessings from God in your lives and in the duty of governing our country.

Thank you.

About the Authors

Ernst Bergen, at age 39, was one of Paraguay's most successful businesspersons. Suddenly, his life took a dramatic turn when he was invited by the incoming President of the country to enter his governing cabinet. Although not a politician, he went on to hold two significant positions: first, Minister of Industry and Commerce, and later, Minister of Finance.

Currently, Ernst and his wife, Lucy, and their three children, live in Asunción, Paraguay. Ernst continues active interest in his businesses and in consulting related to leadership. He remains an active member of Concordia Mennonite Brethren Church in Asunción.

Phyllis Pellman Good is a *New York Times* bestselling author whose books have sold more than 9.5 million books. In addition to the popular *Fix-It and Forget-It* cookbooks, she has written on subjects related to the Amish and Mennonites, on family life, as well as on professionalism.

Phyllis received her B.A. and M.A. in English from New York University. She and her husband, Merle, live in Lancaster, Pennsylvania.